QUILOMBOLA!

Series Editor

LÉONORA MIANO

Quilombola is a Brazilian word for the inhabitant of a maroon, or 'runaway-slave' community. The choice of this appellation is a tribute to those who, throughout human history, have stood up against oppression. However, there is more in this reference: it speaks both about freedom regained and about all the creative gestures that stemmed from that conquest. For those who had broken their chains, the *quilombo* was a place of reappropriation and reinvention of oneself.

It is by inviting writers and readers to practice *marronnage*—'running away from slavery'—of thought, to shift their way of thinking, that the series **Quilombola!** stands out. This list of books is a space from which resonate insubordinate, inventive, provocative and unexpected voices. Whether artists, activists or intellectuals, the authors of **Quilombola!** bring a sensitive reflection on the world and forge new paths. Although focusing on sub-Saharan African and French-speaking Afropean expressions, we welcome minority points of view from other places too.

The series aims at making itself accessible to a large readership in order to promote a wider circulation of thought. It is on this condition that it will come to meaningful fruition.

Blind Spot

MYRIAM TADESSÉ

TRANSLATED BY GILA WALKER

LONDON NEW YORK CALCUTTA

Seagull Books, 2021

Originally written in French as *Point aveugle* by Myriam Tadessé
© Myriam Tadessé, 2021

First published in English translation by Seagull Books, 2021
English translation © Gila Walker, 2021

ISBN 978 0 8574 2 878 3

British Library Cataloguing-in-Publication Data
A catalogue record for this book is available from the British Library

Typeset by Seagull Books, Calcutta, India
Printed and bound by Versa Press, East Peoria, Illinois, USA

Identity is the freedom to be.
Identity is not retreating into sameness.
It is participation in the other.

Edouard Glissant

We tend to think of ourselves as being someone
when at bottom we are several.

Raymond Devos

CONTENTS

There are words that have the effect of grains of sand in a shoe. Words that take you into a minefield, that, hardly have they been pronounced, trigger a series of explosions—cultural, political, philosophical, memorial and emotional.

Like this one: *métis*.

Nothing to do with the dubious use of the term *métissage* held up as banner ads mainly for commercial purposes. No, the word I'm talking about is *métis*, meaning the fact, the state, the person in flesh and soul, which also has nothing to do with the 'crossbreeding of races' in the dictionary.

If I tear race from *métis* as from a sticky bug tape, what would *métis* be the name of? That is what I'm wondering. At any rate, 'that' is what I'm interested in digging into. Seeing what, if anything, it has to do with me.

'One' cannot speak of *the* métis; there are as many *métis* as there are people and spaces. Only 'I' can do so. Fruit of a desire or a constraint, welcomed or rejected, visible or imperceptible, the state of being *métis* is one of disorder. And I would even say, of a crack. Most likely this is why it is so dizzying to try to think it through. Impossible to approach it from the assured categories of history and politics. It is the blind spot.

Something, however, is seeking to be said. Something lurking between the lines of books, of official history, always on the margins, vanishing as soon as we try to look directly at it. Something related to *métissage* and that, rather than designating it, concerns us all.

I've seldom met a well-adjusted *métis*. Is this due to the *métissage* or to a humanity tormented by its demons?

How did I come to understand and realize that I was *métis*? Has it conditioned my way of being in the world and of perceiving it?

The fact of being a *métis* became a subject in the performance world, in the course of my philosophy studies and with my mother, a white Frenchwoman.

It is in light of these three closely intertwined worlds of show business, thought and family that I will try to say something about what it means to be *métis*.

For years I've been looking for a way to tackle this issue. At the end of the day, the answer is simple: right in its heart. It is not outside me since I'm inside it. So it's from this inside, from this experience that I will conduct my reflection.

Being *métis* is not a subject for me. I am the subject of this story.

Representation—Métis *in the Eyes of the Other*

Why not simply try to touch the other,
feel the other, discover each other?

Frantz Fanon, *Black Skin, White Masks*

I'm twenty-five. In my second year of acting studies at Rue Blanche in Paris, I'm bored stiff. Because of my character, ill adapted to institutions, and of the academy itself, which is going through a rough period. The professors who'd inspired in me the desire to go there are gone; those who are left or who've just arrived seem to be there for lack of anything better to do. Everyone is complaining. The students about the administration, about the school's lack of dynamism and a project, and the professors about the students' lack of commitment. In short, I'm immersed in the typically French atmosphere that consists in spending most of one's time and energy grumbling.

Yet, I'd fervently wanted to gain entry to the establishment. My first attempt was seven years earlier, just out of secondary school, before I'd taken a single theatre course. It was the eclecticism of the school that had attracted me then. Ensatt, École Nationale des Arts et Techniques du Théâtre, dubbed Rue Blanche when it was located in Paris, appealed to me with its plurality. All theatrical trades and professions were there, from actors to administration, from scenography to lighting, from costumes to directing. Everything that went into acting, creating, exploring, doing theatre. It spoke of craftsmanship, hands-on experience, the love of a practice. A dream, to my very naive eyes. The very name of the other academy made me wary: Conservatoire National Supérieur d'Art Dramatique struck me as overly dogmatic and pompous to my taste. I didn't understand why it was seen as the Grail. What interest was there in steeping in the vain narcissism of actors alone? I couldn't give a damn about a prestige strategy. I wanted to work in theatre, not develop a career plan.

That first time, I was selected unanimously in the first round but rejected in the second and advised to wait a year, take some courses and try again the following year when, I was assured, I would of course be admitted. Since there were a limited number of openings, the decision had been made to give preference to someone who'd reached the age limit for the competition. I can't say I appreciated it. From my point of view, the argument doesn't hold water. All I understand is they've chosen someone with the same qualifications but who's older. It isn't a good sign that this person, although seven years older, is no better qualified than I. I'm furious, frustrated, stricken with panic. I'd pinned all my hopes on this school, had no fall-back solution, hadn't wanted to even think about it. So be it.

I'll go my way, without them. Let them go take a hike, there will be no next year. Meanwhile, in my pride-filled grief, I am fortunate to benefit from the goodwill of one of the professors who gives me a recommendation for a private course. All I have to do is settle the technical details without delay, enrol in a university to get a scholarship that will serve to pay for the classes.

I decide to turn this failure into an opportunity. It will allow me to roam freely in my own way, off the beaten track, exploring the many paths of theatre to which I'd decided as a very young girl to devote my life. My desire is not limited to being an actor; it extends to all the arts that theatre brings together—literature, dance, music, painting, sculpture and performance. I love it all, I want to do everything—dance, sing, write, act, direct. Everything is related, as my life is to art. Through it, thanks to it, I feel vibrant and alive. Through it, I savour the world and make my way in it. Without limits.

In addition to the Vera Gregh theatre course that the professor advised me to take, I enrol in a class given by Serge Martin, a former professor at the Lecoq school. Two almost diametrically opposed approaches to theatre. One through the text, the other through the body. I like this. For me, they complement each other and there's nothing I fear more than being trapped in a single vision. Also, I very much enjoy being perceived in a contradictory manner. At Vera's, I'm advised to play comic roles in order to curb my tragic temperament. At Serge Martin's, I'm advised to do exactly the opposite. I learn a great deal and work hard at both places. Most of my practice as an actor, I acquire from them, under their benevolent but demanding gaze.

So far so good. No identity walls on the horizon yet. My aspirations float in the warm bubble of the theatre schools and of the classes in the Ethiopian civilization department of the National Institute for Oriental Languages and Civilizations. The only barb comes from my Amharic professor. He's continually challenging me about the meaning of words I'm supposed to know, since I'm Ethiopian. His foolish complacency reminds me of the attitude of the professors at the lycée in Addis Ababa who'd put me off studying my paternal tongue. More profoundly, it awakens a secret wound that I was trying to heal by going to these classes. That of not speaking my father's language. I have the structure, music and spirit of it, but my vocabulary is so limited that I'm left standing at the threshold of speech. The language of my native land knocks about inside me as if I were a skeleton endowed with a heart but without the flesh or muscles that would allow it to expose itself. Nonetheless, to carry a 'silenced' language within me, to borrow the term used by Alice Cherki,[1] has less to do with a lack of words than with a lack of people speaking them. Mastering a language, especially one's own, is not simply a matter of vocabulary, that is, of technical proficiency. More vitally, it is a personal history. An interweaving of emotions, affective memory and relationships. This is probably why it's so painful to learn one's own language. You don't rush into it, as you would into a foreign language, towards the other who enriches you by opening you up to other perceptions of the world. You're pressing where it hurts. The inconsolable lack of what's been taken from you because of the failure to transmit it.

---

1 Alice Cherki, *La frontière invisible* (Paris: Éditions des crépuscules, 2008).

The professor's remarks wouldn't have affected me so deeply if they hadn't revived the words a classmate had once thrown in my face. I had just dropped out of the Amharic classes given to Ethiopian students at the Franco-Ethiopian lycée of Addis Ababa. Unlike my classmates, who suffered as much as I did from the incompetence of the professors who spent hours dictating pages of grammar they themselves didn't understand, I didn't speak Amharic at home. My father had never addressed a word to me in any language other than French. As for my cousins, they opted as I did for the language of their education, in their case English. When it came to this, the 1974 Ethiopian Revolution didn't help matters. My family was scattered around the world, my father imprisoned, my grandmother walled herself up in silence. I was left alone with my mother. I was nine, thirteen when I gave up taking the classes. This classmate of mine, whom I considered a friend, rebuked me. 'You're repudiating your blood.' Of course, I felt I had to defend myself, to counter her and bring to bear all the meagre rationality of a child dealing with thoughts beyond her ken. I can't recall exactly what I said and it doesn't really matter. I simply remember it made a big hole inside me and that I cried that night in the darkness of my bedroom for a long time. I'd just experienced what would make my strength and my solitude, the loss of a sense of belonging to a community.

How they pissed me off with what I was supposed to be, to know, to represent! The expression is coarse on purpose. It suits the intrusive vulgarity of those who dictate in your stead what you should be. Assigning your identity to a function. To be sure, this is not, alas, limited to the *métis*. Nothing is. What I mean is that the issues the *métis* has to grapple with are the lot of all human beings, except they are so in double measure. Being a *métis* means not being able to escape them. For better or for worse.

No doubt this was not unrelated to the joy, not to mention the relief, I felt to journey inside others. How good it was to be able to hang your hat in a place and one place only, without being torn by several parts all claiming their primacy. To be nothing but this, a character, complex and contradictory, whose only affiliation is with the words of a poet. To have to attend to this only, to exist in the moment, without attachments, without fetters, without a trace of blood.

But let's return to this point in my story, my first year of professional acting studies. I'm eighteen, and until then—it is worth pointing out—the question of my skin colour and my phenotype has not come up. Not even for the smallest fraction of a second. Nothing. It has never even crossed my mind.

So much so that when, at the end of the course year, I get a call from the Black Theatre for an audition, I hardly pay attention to the term 'Black'. What I hear is theatre and the possibility of acting. This is the only thing that interests me.

At the time—we're in 1983—the Black Theatre had moved to the twelfth arrondissement in Paris. Four years after its founding by Benjamin Jules-Rosette and Darling Légitimus as a simple troop in 1975, it had become a cultural ensemble with its own venue and the capacity to host and promote other artists of the French-speaking Afro-Caribbean region. Its vocation and what motivated its creation is to offer 'Black artists a tribune for common expression'.[2] A 'tribune', the term is not insignificant: related as it is etymologically to tribunal, and thus to politics and political discourse, it straightaway positions the adventure of the theatre in terms of a demand to be seen and heard in a space that does not otherwise permit it. It points to a problem that is still ours today, namely, the discrepancy between the plurality of French society and its representation in the theatre.

I know nothing of all this when I walk into the Black Theatre. All I know, all I see, is that it is a place dedicated to West Indian and African playwrights and poets, that the director and manager is West Indian, and the actors too. And so what? What could be more natural? I see this not as a sign of a 'problem' but as a source of richness. Of sensibilities, expressions, outlooks. These aren't 'Blacks'—that means nothing to me; they are West Indian artists whom I don't know and am curious to meet. My only concern is artistic in nature, and the early moments of the audition give me cause for concern.

The premiere of the play *À petit feu de chagrin*, a poetic montage adapted from Georges Desportes' *Cette île qui est la nôtre*, is to take place in two weeks and the two main and only actors are gone. Benjamin Jules-Rosette, the director and author of the adaptation, is going to take over the male role; they need an actor for the female character. None of this is a good sign, but, after all, their disagreements are not my affair and I find the situation amusing. Let's see if I can rise to the challenge and if it's worth it. The boss seems very friendly. I read the adaptation, find it perplexing, listen courteously

2 Sall Amadou Lamine, 'La tyrannie du théâtre ou la quête métisse de Benjamin Jules-Rosette' in Benjamin Jules-Rosette, *Itinéraire du Théâtre Noir* (Paris: l'Harmattan 1999), p. 9.

to his somewhat confused directions, do the best I can. We shake hands. It's a deal. I'm to start two days later, the time it will take to work on the text at home.

I'd rather not dwell on the bewildering rehearsals—my partner mixes up the scenes and replies. I say to myself that at least I'll have learnt what not to do. The show itself is a fiasco. We have to cancel performances for lack of an audience. I discover the joys of Ti' Punch, but begin worrying that if it goes on like this, with me spending my nights at the bar drinking rather than on stage, I'll end up an alcoholic. It seems that the glory days of the Black Theatre are over. The director is pissed off and blames everyone for the failure, to begin with the public itself. But why should they come if it's bad (and indeed it is)? Out of community solidarity? All this leaves me dubious, which the director notices and doesn't appreciate one bit. Clearly, our relations are not the most cordial. What of it? I sign on again for another play, *Le paysage de l'aveugle*, based on the work by Émile Ollivier. It would be a shame, I think, to give up so quickly, before having met the troupe. I want to work, I need to work, to be with actors. What's more, the text does not leave the rebel in me indifferent. To speak of revolution in the language of poets is right up my alley. Nonetheless, I know this show will be my last. I will have to leave if I want to make progress. I suffer, I must admit, from the carelessness of the staging. I can't help it, that's how I am and will remain throughout my career. I have the eye of a director and can't confine myself to playing my part without paying attention to the rest. Doing my own thing well with no regard for the big picture doesn't interest me nor does it make any sense to me. An instrumentalist who plays on tune in an orchestra that is poorly conducted and sounds out of tune can do nothing to make the music better. And that is what matters, the music, not the musician's ego. In short, the dissensions around this second play are no better than before: to the contrary, there are even more of them. But this time, the public does show up, and at least I have the joy of being able to move them.

Being moved. Isn't that what's essential? What's the point of good intentions and lofty speeches if we can't achieve this mysterious, impalpable thing that makes us vibrant and hence alive? Isn't this what enables us to break through boundaries, as woefully aggravating as they may be? Isn't this what the artist has the privilege of inhabiting and the responsibility for offering, like 'an axe for the frozen sea inside us'?[3]

What I lacked here was the high standards for achieving this emotion which, in the theatre, takes the form of an aesthetic approach, a discipline of the body and the mind, to best convey a text's vibration. I sought to magnify and transfigure, but I came up against illustrative stagings, underscoring the affects instead of bringing to the surface the dynamics that make the beauty and complexity of humankind.

Having said that, my intention is not to denigrate the great adventure of the Black Theatre and the importance it may have had. I'm speaking here in the concrete terms of my concerns, at the time, focused as they are on the stage and what could be invented there. I am confronted with specific, practical questions, and can't be bothered with ideological intentions, no matter how appealing.

---

3 Frantz Kafka, letter to Oskar Pollack, 27 January 1904, in *Letters to Friends, Family, and Editors* (Richard and Clara Winston trans) (New York: Schocken, 1977), p. 16.

And to be perfectly frank, what I actually see is artistic carelessness and a struggle of egos masked by lofty discourse. My concerns are at once more down-to-earth and idealistic. How and where to find the theatre I'm dreaming of? What could it be like? I couldn't define it then and am equally incapable of doing so today. At best, I could attach some adjectives to it, liken it to one tradition rather than another. You have to come across it to know it. Like love. Neither exists already formed somewhere. They are invented, constructed, experienced in a practice, in the relationship with another and, in this case, with a director and his universe. One thing was certain, at any rate: promoting a cultural identity was not my concern. Conversing with others was; belonging to a community was not. Besides, I didn't even know what that could mean. In the sense of an identity, in any case. Was this due to my status as a *métis*, to my personal background, or to both? Assuming that one can be distinguished from the other. Assuming further that my questions at the time could be posed in such terms. The fact is, and I must insist on this point, this wasn't the case. The questions I may have had at the time, and of course I did, were all focused on my path as an actor.

As I've said, I saw theatre as encompassing several modes of expression between which I wouldn't have wanted or known how to choose. Being an actor let me embrace them all. I didn't see it as a profession, in the sense of a skill that lets you earn a living or a way of being in the world when you don't really know what to do with yourself. It was more of an apprenticeship, a navigation channel through emotions, languages, stories and spaces. A passage, that I thought of as such and not as an end in itself. My aspiration was to make films, to write and direct. To meet my stories . . .

In the meantime, I put an end to the Black Theatre episode, start exploring movement through different forms of dance and Aikido, go to the theatre a lot and, prompted by my fellow students in the Vera Gregh class, stage Michel de Ghelderode's *Escurial*. I experiment, learn, explore. I suffer setbacks too, with the *mise-en-scène* crew but especially when the head of the Black Theatre takes a cheap shot at me and calls off a meeting with Peter Brook, the director of my dreams at the time. But those are the vicissitudes of life and of my profession which have nothing yet to do with any particular condition. 'Colour is not a human or a personal reality; it is a political reality,' James Baldwin wrote.[4] So far, this political reality does not affect me. I know it exists, but it's not part of my story. Why should it be? I don't live in South Africa or in the United States, but in France, in Paris, which I see as a city that is open to the world. I'm often asked about my origins, but I see this as simple curiosity on the part of people I don't resemble. I'm not conditioned to be perceived or to see others through the prism of racial discrimination.

Yet something is amiss. Something that comes less from the story I've been telling so far than from the way I've been telling it. As if I were swimming against the tide of my own story and the one others would like to hear. This insistence on removing my experience as a *métis* from the racial question with which it is usually coupled ends up pointing to it again and again. Is this because it is the required paradigm without which the designation of *métis* itself would not exist? No doubt, but it is too early at this stage to discuss whether or not the term needs to be changed when one

---

4 James Baldwin, *The Fire Next Time* (London: Dial Press, 1963), p. 110.

doesn't recognize oneself in its presuppositions. The question is complex, insofar as it concerns as much the history of the word, its manufacture and what it produces in turn, as the state of mind conditioned to think in terms of classification.

But there is a paradox that I feel I should specify at present because it designates the tension that conditions this narrative. The paradox between the intimate place from which I speak, who I am, and my social environment. Even if I think of myself outside 'racial' categories, I cannot disregard the fact that my story and the process of writing it are confronted with them. No matter how much I insist on being the subject of my story, from the moment I articulate it through this *métis* lens, the *I* in question finds itself put through the grinder of the presuppositions induced by the society in which I find myself. The personal reality from which I speak and want to speak is filling with water from all sides, like a frail vessel tossed by the storms of history.

It's a fact, like it or not, that there is an obligation in France to go through the channel of discrimination to speak of difference. Either it exists and it is always based on a problem, or it is denied, which is another problem. So I'm led, despite myself, to begin by positioning myself in relation to a gaze that sees me in negative. In the photographic sense of the term. There is no way out of this, once I use the name by which it designates me. A priori at least.

This is why, before proceeding further, it seems important to me to dwell for a moment on this paradox. All the more so since I've chosen to undertake this exploration in the open, that is, based on my own experience, without hiding behind any 'knowledge' of the subject.

So let's go back to my story. I'm twenty, in my second year in philosophy, living a great love, keeping at my Aikido classes although they're not very good, and my pockets are just about filled from a recently shot film in which I had a part. My first. Noticed and appreciated by the film crew, I am promised a great future. It's not long in coming. My agent, ecstatic, calls to tell me that a great casting bigwig has heard about me, seen my photos, and, before even meeting me, has declared that I am to be THE female protagonist in the next Jean-Jacques Beineix movie. I must get the book on which the screenplay is based right away, to get an idea of 'my' character ('You'll see, it's grreeat'), before the imminent meeting with the bigwig. I do as I'm told, read the book, don't find it as great as all that but not without interest, begin dreaming of the character and meet the big wheel. Delighted to meet me, compliments, blah blah, the deal seems as good as done. I will still have to see the director, a meeting which, needless to say, will take place very soon. Time goes by. I'm worried. They reassure me, the director is thinking. Okay. I believe what I'm told. I don't yet know how to read between the lines. Second or third interview with the bigwig, and this time the enthusiasm has dropped considerably. This thing that makes people squirm on their seat, between discomfort and annoyance, indifference and pity, the how can I put it . . .

' . . . the director doesn't want a *métis* for the role.'

The first explosion of this word. A word I never suspected could fall on me like an axe.

What came before or after, I can't recall. Probably some sugar-coating, a little flattery here, some encouragement there. All I remember is this, this sentence, the word *métis* that I was hearing for the first time in that way, holding the leading, principal, unique role, and that cast me, my person, the young actor, with her sensibility, her personality, her style . . . out somewhere. Where? I don't know. But not where I thought I was in any case. What's more, I no longer existed. I had the brutal sensation of being wiped off the map. It's the risk of the acting profession, which is not really a profession in the sense that it isn't a mere mastery of technical skills that one offers but one's very self, an ability to navigate into others and make them exist with one's own body. The boundary between the self, one's intimate being, and the skill at interpreting the words of others is so tenuous and fluctuating that it leaves you naked. In the final analysis, when you are refused a role, you can't but be physically affected, thinking that it's you who is not wanted, turning it into an existential drama. Even when you try to laugh about it and not give it too much importance, every rejection is nevertheless a blow that, when struck time and again, ultimately leaves you in pieces. This is the risk, indeed, a correlative of the very nature of this strange exercise of existing only in and through the gaze of others.

What happened that time, that first time, was different in nature. It wasn't the *no* that struck me in the face, it was what motivated that *no*. And that made me implode. Like rape. Torn from the inside.

'Don't worry about it. You'll be working a lot, that's for sure. You're a star. I know what I'm talking about, you'll see.' Gimme a break! Dumbfounded, I kept silent, took it all in, the bitter and the sweet, upright, bolt upright, to the point of stiffness, my posture and smile imperturbable. A matter of upbringing. Dignity and elegance at all times, even more a Pavlovian reflex than a value at this stage. I never saw my elders on their knees, fissured inside, to be sure, but always erect.

It was in the privacy of my bedroom that I broke down. I didn't understand, no I didn't understand what I'd just heard. If he'd told me I no longer corresponded to the character as the director now saw her, I could have accepted it. I would have been disappointed, angry no doubt, because I'd have felt like a toy in the hands of a whimsical child. Why tell me yes, sure thing, when they really weren't sure at all. I would have taken it for thoughtlessness, tactlessness, a total lack of professionalism. There's no law against doubting but it would have been the least of courtesies to say so. Or yet again, if I'd gone for a screen test that wasn't up to the mark, I would have acquiesced. I would have blamed myself for not being convincing enough. But I was eliminated not on the basis of my acting skills or my temperament, but because the director didn't want a '*métis*'? What could that possibly mean? If I understood correctly, what they saw on my photos was not a face, with what it reveals about a personality, a sensibility, and hence about a person, but a '*métis*'. Here I was, suddenly a 'race', a specimen of another species, a thing stored in a box. If I understood correctly, or not, I didn't want it: I wasn't an actor capable of playing a character but a *métis*.

Meaning what?

I was to find out from subsequent castings. No matter how hard I refused to let myself be stopped by their outcome, attributing it each time to the particular, personal stupidity of the given inter-locutor, I was faced with the same immutable sentence: 'Too Black; not Black enough; you don't fit any category.' The undefined colour of my skin was sweeping away my dreams, projects, efforts as if by a tsunami, when I thought I was meeting artists and being judged on the merits of my talents as an actor. Feather after feather, I had no choice but to fold my wings. There was no place for me. No pro-vision in the programme. Like an exotic object on a flat encephalo-gram, there at best to enhance the colour of the living-room curtains. Willingly even. But as an actor, with a text to say and something to play. There are limits to how far a person can be pushed. Already for the others, the 'normal' actors, it wasn't easy, so obviously shit-stirrers upsetting the great order of civilizations should expect to shut up and look pretty. And incidentally, the invariable and only piece of casting advice I ever received from my various agents was: 'Make sure you go looking very pretty.'

The selection criteria, based on racial phenotype, opened my eyes to a reality that I'd naively believed to be that of apartheid South Africa. What wasn't laid down in laws could be read in the scenarios and in the eyes of directors. No need to saddle yourself with psychology, craftsmanship, or even a minimum of character. There were the 'normal' roles and there were the others, and on the rare occasions when the latter existed, they were described with a laconic 'Black man or woman'. I was presumed to be Black because of my African ancestry; my skin wasn't black, but I had features too distinctive to be white. So at the end of the day, I was nothing. A dead angle. 'You could play any role!' they'd assure me with a broad smile. Any, and hence none in particular. They could just as easily have said: 'Come back when you've made the effort to correspond to something definite. Be Black with black skin or white with white features. Period.' But to state frankly what these criteria implied would have meant to be aware of it and assume responsibility for it. And nobody wanted to do so. It would have meant recognizing the shameful stench of colonialism. So it was always the other person who was the idiot, who was guilty of ridiculous, simplistic prejudices. The agents pointed their finger at casting directors who blamed the writers and directors who accused the producers who placed responsibility squarely on the public's shoulders, that were broad enough, of course. It was their role.

As for my roles, I saw them melt away like snow in the sun. The famous 'inner sun' that many of my compatriots in exoticism are said to have and that we are supposed to 'pull out' like a rabbit from a magician's hat. For those of you who are not in the know, let me clarify how things work. You're hired to play role X on TV movie Y. You ask the director a question about your part. Don't quibble about gender. Male, female, the treatment is no different. Same thing for colour: half Black or a hundred per cent Black, it doesn't matter. You're Black, period. Which means spontaneous, exuberant and joyful—at least at the time I'm talking about, in the late eighties and early nineties, you are not readily shown pulling a long face—yet you persist in thinking of yourself as an actor and you ask the question. There, with a broad grin—it's crazy how contagious African energy can be—the director replies: 'Don't worry, pull out your inner sun and it'll be just fine.' The wording may vary slightly (why don't you ... it's all about ... c'mon just ...), the inner sun, never. Written into the corpus of directing 'Black' actors. The first time, it's surprising, no doubt about it. Some actors, and this was my case, are so rattled, they gulp and swallow their supposed inner sun whole. Mustn't show you're upset, focus on your heating bill and recite a mantra to yourself. Here's my personal favourite, from Guillaume Apollinaire's poem 'Song of the Ill Loved' in *Alcools*:

> Rotting Salonika fish
> Necklace of bad dreams
> Of eyes removed with skewers
> Your mother floated a mephitic fart
> And from her colic you were born[5]

It will not answer your question, but it allows you to keep your sun on the inside.

Once the initial shock is over, this status of *métis* begins to interest me. So I don't fit into existing categories, all the better. I was not born to be boxed in and I don't see my existence as having to serve degraded and degrading imaginaries. My disappointment is, after all, only the consequence of my idealism. I'm learning the contingencies of the profession, which should be taken for what they are, and by no means as determinant. The stupidity and mediocrity encountered in the audiovisual world dragging its soul, between the brainless narcissism of most actors and the smugness of directors with nothing to say, cannot define the whole profession. Concentrate on what I want. I have faith in life, in human beings, that's where I stand, singlemindedly, wholeheartedly. Enrich myself with cinema, real cinema, watching, observing, learning from those

---

5 Guillaume Apollinaire, *Selected Poems* (Martin Sorrell trans.) (London: Oxford University Press, 2015), p. 27.

I admire, love and aspire to join. It's all a matter of meeting the right person, eventually the right one will come along. There will be wonderful, passionate encounters, like those with Peter Brook and Gary Hill. The problem is they lead nowhere. Things don't mesh, as they say, the engine starts turning, but each time it stalls as it's about to take off. Neither my work nor my conduct are in question. On the contrary, both are strongly appreciated. But in the end, there seems to be something exceptional about the exercise of my profession, in two ways: first the roles for which I can qualify are rare, and my personality, described as uncommon, aggravates my case. 'What do you want? It's not that I haven't proposed you and shown your photos, but each time it's the same story. They stop at your picture, sigh and end up saying, a shame but she's too good. With her looks and personality, she's made for playing lead roles. The problem is that there are none for people like her,' my agent explains when I complain about the dearth of auditions. And the times when, at my insistence, an audition was set up for what was described as a bit part or a supporting role—I wanted to act and refused to be weighed down by such terms, considering, as Brecht said, that there are no small parts, just small actors—I'd find myself sharply rebuffed: 'What are you doing here? Have you taken a look at yourself? The role of a vulgar prostitute is not for you! Also, you have more presence than the leading actor! No, you have no business being here.'

Sometime later, the same casting director, who'd called me in for a part for which I should have been suited this time, since it was to play an Ethiopian, rebuffed me just as sharply because I 'didn't look Ethiopian [*sic*]'. Flustered, as if I'd been caught doing something wrong, I began to excuse myself for being only 'half'

Ethiopian, which would account for what she was accusing me of. 'But no, you're not Ethiopian at all, since you don't look like this photo.' Again *sic*, alas. And she showed me a picture of an Ethiopian taken from goodness knows which anthropology book. No need for me to dwell on the state of shock mixed with anger into which her remark threw me. What's important to point out is that this person was not only an established figure in the film world—cultivated, intelligent and what have you—she also knew me and appreciated me very much. The same woman fought tooth and nail for me to play a character of Haitian origin in a Canadian series, insulting the producer, calling him a moron for not wanting me because I was not an authentic Haitian. So after I exhaled and took another breath, I asked her if she had been looking for an English woman and the actor who showed up was a red-head while the one on the photo was blonde, would she have proclaimed, with equal confidence, that she couldn't be English since she didn't correspond to a photo defining the essential blondness of the English? 'Am I auditioning for a role or for an ethnology catalogue?' She looked at me, dumbstruck. I left with her apologies which, as usual, consisted in hanging it all on these directors with no imagination. Ultimately, the part was given to a woman who was neither Ethiopian nor an actor but a famous model, and later they came pleading to me to dub her. Her utter lack of talent, as if by magic, brought me back into the identity of an Ethiopian actor.

Nonetheless, I didn't kick up an identity fuss about it. I was confronted with real problems, serious ones, some having to do with me as a person, others with a series of prejudices that *enclosed* it, to be sure, but with I refused to make into *a* problem. In other words, to let myself be defined by it. I positioned myself not as a *métis*, but as an actor, and persisted in wanting to be hired on the basis of my skills, not my type. The whole thing seemed clearly compromised in cinema, overly constrained by some degree of naturalism and imperatives of plausibility. The implausible here being to disregard 'race' and the way its manufacture had forged imaginaries. Without a role specifically written for a *métis*, my chances of having a part in a movie were slim. And even if one turned up, my *métissage* would have to correspond to what the writer and director had in mind. This piling up of projections, presuppositions and prejudices left little room for the humanity of the character, let alone that of the actor. I can't even say it denied the humanity, since, for this to be the case, it would have had to exist. And that was precisely the problem. The making of this type of character was flawed from the start, so much so that the question of its humanity and hence its complexity did not even arise. It was reduced to a type—a figure, not a subject. I couldn't help but notice that its existence was connected to an absence of colour. Like in a game of musical chairs, chromatic chairs in this case, it sufficed for a colour to appear for it to take the place of the person. Being a person of colour cast you out of humanity, which refrained from naming itself by its complexion, since doing so would have broken its stranglehold on the game and reduced it to the rank of a colour among others. An affair of domination, played out and organized by a command of the naming process, but which I didn't see as such at the time. Not accepting oneself as white while imposing on others to be Black was a way of masking the absurdity and poverty of the conversation:

—So you're Black?

—Yes, so they say. And you, you're white?

Well, isn't that simply fascinating? As for confusing the two, don't even think about it—nobody dared. Insofar as I was concerned, the matter was settled: there was no provision for me in the audiovisual conversation and I had no desire to participate in it. There was still the theatre, which was no minor thing to have left, since this was what I wanted most. Shakespeare, Sophocles, Chekhov, those whose plays I'd explored in my studies and who'd given me a taste for texts. The problem was getting into it. Auditions took place in closed circles, and my agent was only ever solicited by a private theatre looking for an exotic actor to play a comedy of no interest. In the end, I realized that the only way to get into the theatre world was to go through the network of national schools of theatrical arts. There wasn't a chance I'd be noticed by a director in the state of invisibility in which I found myself. That's how I decided to take the entrance exams to Rue Blanche again. I desperately needed to be somewhere.

So here I am, after a long detour, at Rue Blanche where I'm bored. This somewhere that allowed me to be hired to work on a play, to be seen again as an actor and not as an exotic thing, where everything could turn out for the best but nothing was going well at all. It's not so much that I'm bored, I'm suffocating. Cramped, out of place, incongruous? Out of my element in any case. In a year, I've exhausted what the school could offer me, in terms of education and developing contacts. Though all the different professions are represented, everyone is moving in their own orbit. The synergy I was dreaming of doesn't take hold. Actor, sure, but to say what and with whom? What seemed obvious to me is not at all so any more. Something is always missing, a sense, substance, a vision. Working on beautiful texts is good. But what then? I see that the school, because of its location, will not be the springboard I was hoping for. I realize, especially, after the play that this place offered me the chance to work on and which had restored my hope, that I am and remain above all someone different, an exotic.

'You'll make a magnificent Bérénice,' the director had said when he hired me. As if he were dangling a carrot before my eyes. It was a play he'd put on afterwards . . . for me of course. Flattering as it was, the proposal made me uncomfortable. On the one hand, I could 'see myself already'. On the other, I wondered what could possibly be the point. Was this what I was looking for? To 'make' a magnificent Bérénice, or any other character for that matter? And why this need to hold out promises? I had enough to do with the small role he'd given me right now: Panope, the humble lady-in-waiting in *Phèdre* by Racine, because I also had to choreograph dance sequences for between the acts. The challenge was to find a meaningful form that would simultaneously propel and translate the play's tragic movement. At least that's how I'd understood the rather vague idea he'd submitted to me. I worked hard, too happy to be able to invent, to participate in the making of a performance with artists whom I admired. Once again, however, despite the success, my work will remain without effect.

No amount of good will on my part could change a thing: I sense that I'm disturbing. Like a strand of hair in a bowl of soup. Something is also starting to bother me. A hiatus that had not particularly attracted my attention until now, having to do not so much with a given audition, a given director or a given school as with the society in which I lived, and its mentality.

I'd regarded Paris as a cultural crossroads, because here you could see movies, shows, listen to music, read books from around the world. I hadn't realized how impervious it remained to people living there. Where were those whom I thought I'd seen but who actually remained invisible, or so little visible, present only on an exceptional basis, as if passing through, in short, out of place? Where were my different others? Because now that the question had been brought up and that I myself was bringing it up, I began to feel very much alone. Nobody around me, in the theatre world, wanted to hear about it. It's not that it disturbed them; they simply rejected it out of hand. Null and void. A problem? What problem? I was imagining things, projecting my personal difficulty onto society. A problem? Everyone had problems! 'When they don't want you, they always find something to say. With you, it's that you're neither Black nor white; with me, it's that my nose is too big [*sic*].' The absurdity of the argument, recurrent and delivered in good faith, left me speechless. What can you say to people who don't even realize that they're equating something that can be considered a physical defect, even if it's silly, even if it stems from arbitrary aesthetic criteria, with being a *métis* or Black or yellow, or anything other than white? Did I really have to explain that it wasn't a physical defect?

Everyone was moving in their own orbit. Now I felt isolated rather than alone. Was this what it was like being a *métis* in France? Having no place?

II

At Home Where?

Blue sand
where did you come from?
Last night the rain fell
and it released you

Are you a Cuban woman?
No, I'm not a Cuban woman
Are you a Jarocha woman?
No, I'm not a Jarocha woman
What would you like to be?
I'm a butterfly

Lila Downs, 'Arenita azul', based on the traditional
Mexican song 'Soy el negro de la costa'.

April 1978. A young girl stands, ramrod straight in front of unfa-
miliar faces. They observe her in silence. 'Let me introduce your
new classmate.' The principal's voice reaches her from a distance
behind her heart banging in her head. Whispers, some stifled

laughter. It's her coat, they must be laughing at the ugliness of this chequered thing that compresses her. She feels ridiculous, old-fashioned, held in. If only she could take it off, go sit with the others, not be exposed to their mocking gaze. She's scared, sweats from shyness, feels trapped in this room with its piss-yellow walls. There are bars on the windows, how horrid those bars, is this a prison or what, and the teacher, she's dry and insipid, everyone looks drab, even the students, they all have the same greyish face, just like the windows looking out onto a grey that's not even grey, a lack of colour everywhere, from floor to ceiling to the entrance gate, the street, all colourless. 'She's from Ethiopia,' it feels weird to her to hear this word coming from the outside, when she always heard it inside her, in Amharic, and now it sounds like a foreign country, an abstract, distant entity, a lesson in geography, size-population-climate, an all-consuming over-there that defines it as away-from-here, but here, where is it? What does she know of countries, she doesn't come from Ethiopia, she had to leave it, she comes from a family, a house, a city, a past torn to shreds. France, she doesn't know either, Paris, yes, her grandmother and her aunt, yes, the imitation lace oilcloth on the table, macaroni with grated Gruyere cheese, the Disney films she'd go to see on Christmas with her mother, the bouts of bronchitis because she was sure to catch a cold after a museum visit, the yellow of Van Gogh. Here, it was holiday time, a short stay, passing through, and now . . . now it's over. She can go sit down. Darkness.

Her first class at Lycée Jules-Ferry, Paris, eighteenth arrondissement, Place de Clichy Métro station. It's snowing. Bell rings. The other students leap up, laugh, call out to one another, she stays seated. A boy pops up in front of her, a globe in his arms, thumps it down on her desk, puts Africa right under her nose and orders: 'Show me! Where's Ethiopia?' Short, brown hair, the surly look of the very shy, but eyes sparkling with curiosity. She complies. He stares at the point with such concentration that she feels like he's actually travelling across the country. Satisfied, he picks up the globe and disappears as suddenly as he'd appeared. Darkness.

The silent melancholy of a young girl in the spring light and the beginning of a friendship on the steps of the school. Fog.

Paris starts at the movie theatre. A beaming moon winks at me, a cloud turns into a razor blade and slices an eyeball, a Pierrot frantically calls his beloved as she's swallowed up by the carnival crowd. I'm submerged in a stream of marvellous, terrifying, uncanny images. An unsuspected world opens up to me, calls me, sweeps me away. I want to be among them, to stay with these bold, fanciful characters, who play with their lives as if they were tossing balls in a juggling act. Light. The old man with a bald round head sitting next to me smiles at me. 'It's Marcel Carné,' whispers my mother who came with me for this tribute to Méliès. My first evening out since we came to Paris a few months ago. I owe it to a thoughtful neighbour of my aunt, the grandson of Méliès. Champagne, petits fours and shows of respect. At thirteen, I may be young, but I know the misery hidden behind the decorative lights. This may even be the first characteristic of my *métissage*. This ability to see under the surface of people from here or there, being as I am part of here and there. Of both continents, social classes, worlds, time frames *at once*, I have a twofold gaze. Who knows, on that evening, for instance, and who cares, how the great Méliès's grandson lives? People greet him, congratulate him for his precious contribution to the evening, he looks proud, happy, and yet . . . . What I see is the sadness in his eyes, the insecurity of an operetta singer from another time, another age, that no one listens to any more, which is what leads him to have to walk through my aunt's apartment every evening, when he's not on the road, to get to his 'maid's room', reiterating how sorry he is for the inconvenience. In the thick fog of those first months through which I move like a robot, it is to this gentle, shy, old man, with his beige overcoat and plaid scarf, that I owe my first dream of cinema and my first glimmer of hope. Ever since I'm here, living at my aunt's, 58 Rue Caulaincourt, not on holiday, not passing through on my way to Addis Ababa, but waiting to find a place to live, because there will be no going back, everything has become alien and distant to me. I'm somewhere else. An elsewhere of experience rather than of geography. The split caused by a revolution that shook up the course of my life and my outlook on the world around me.

Until then, I had a mother and a father. It didn't matter to me that they were from here or from there, that they did this or that. They were my papa and my mama, the guardians and providers of my existence on earth. Until then, I had a land, a house, a family and friends. I lived in a world made of presences. They could be close or distant, real or invisible, human, animal, plant, mineral, earthly or celestial—they were, that's all. The expression, the manifestation of a world that they structured in return and of which I was a part. The first effect of the revolution, for me as a child, was not only to disrupt the coexistence of these presences, and even more of human beings, but also their very nature. Now, instead of existing in an unalienable relationship to life, they somehow became dependent on arbitrary circumstances. Ideology had replaced human relations, dividing human beings between those who killed and those who were killed, in the name of a word—revolution—the meaning of which no one could agree on. At first, I'd associated it with a storm and the way in which it could be both frightening and exciting. It swept away what had to die and made way for a new, more just world to emerge. As weeks, then months, then years went by, what I saw was blood, torture, arrests. Brother against brother, sister against sister, children against their parents, terror, families torn apart, denouncing each other, murdering each other. The revolution, like a Moloch, demanded evermore blood and traitors, spread suspicion, vengeance, jealousy, greed, score-settling. A thirst for power. Were sentiments merely a matter of circumstance, a fool's game controlled by puppeteers? What was this world where anything and its opposite could be said, where two plus two was equivalent to whatever the powerful decided according to their interests? I learnt to listen and watch. The person behind the discourse, the private motives behind acts.

I learnt about solitude. After my father was arrested, many of those who considered themselves my friends at school thought it better to have nothing to do with me. Hardly anybody came over to see us at home. The family was dislocated, some were in exile or in prison, others walled up in their grief. I learnt to trust the wind. It took what needed to be swept away and brought new seeds. Other friendships developed, deeper and more meaningful, but which remained, for me, restricted to the premises of the school. Spaces were divided and self-contained. Home, school, my grandmother's place, the weekly market, prison. Going from one to another was a test of strength. The city streets were occupied by tanks and patrols of soldiers threatened at any moment to turn them into traps. The slightest movement, look or attitude that could draw attention to you could be fatal. People locked themselves up at home but still didn't feel safe. Searches, raids for no reason at all, at any hour of the day or night. And yet what I felt was rage rather than fear. At being confined, oppressed, powerless. In the prevailing atmosphere of uncertainty and arbitrariness, I took refuge in the inviolate space of dreams, music and literature. Not being able to move freely in real space, I travelled the world through my parent's library. There, I was no longer isolated. My emotions, my questions encountered others that extended, nurtured and developed them from different perspectives. I grew up very quickly, all too quickly, and if I suffered from the gap between me and others, it was not because of the limping of sorts that is usually attached to the '*métis*' due to some intrinsic duality, but because of a maturity beyond my biological age. It was when I arrived in France that I became especially aware of this. As long as I was with my own people, meaning people who shared the same experience of dictatorship, I hadn't felt this quite as acutely. What I'd suffered from, on the other hand, what had revolted me, was the injustice towards my Ethiopian classmates. The revolution had split the Addis lycée into two camps that had been united until then, or at least I thought they had.

Located in the heart of the capital, on Avenue Churchill, the city's main artery, Lycée Guebre-Mariam of Addis Ababa was a microcosm in itself. Unlike French lycées, the classes ran from kindergarten up through the end of secondary school. Because we spent so much time there, from childhood until we were young adults, it obviously held a central place in all our lives. Addis Ababa was a cosmopolitan city. Headquarters of the Organisation of African Unity (OAU), founded in 1963 by Emperor Haile Selassie, and, starting in the 1920s, a sanctuary for refugees from Orthodox

Armenian, Russian and Greek communities because of the Coptic religion, the capital also had an Indian population invited by Emperor Menelik to contribute to the edification of the capital, and a sizeable Italian community, a vestige of the occupation, that had grown attached to the country. No less than fifty nationalities grew up together at the lycée. Last but not least, the school was free and hence accessible to all social classes.

So it wasn't an establishment reserved for expatriate elites, the offspring of ambassadors and high-ranking government officials. This was where I spent my first years as a young adult, with no distinctions of class, race or gender. I'm not saying that differences didn't exist. Simply that the emphasis was on what brought us together, a single space, the same education and treatment in a common language. Personally I don't recall there having been groups based on class or national affiliation before the revolution. The school was far from a self-contained entity; in fact, what I loved about it was how it opened me up to the world. With the revolution, it split into two clans. On one side, the privileged expatriate community that continued to live in a bubble, untouched by the events, and, on the other, the Ethiopians. The teachers changed too. Many left the country and the new ones had all the traits of mercenaries. They seemed to have come only for the sake of financial gain, the comfortable bonus for teaching in a dangerous territory. Indifferent to the country, they didn't want to hear about the troubles that many of the Ethiopian students were facing. One of them went so far as to punish a student for not doing his homework when everyone knew it was because he had spent the night in jail. At least on that case, I was able to do something. I organized a strike to denounce the outrageous attitude of these professors and, since I was a good student, the administration supported us. Nevertheless, I came to detest most of the French; I say most because there were some wonderful people among them, but the rest were conspicuous in their arrogance and indifference to others, adults and students alike. Even my mother, who was French and had seen a lot in her time, was stunned by the attitude of her compatriots. One day, she'd confided her worries about the political situation to one of them, only to hear her reply with utmost earnestness: 'Yes, things are really terrible. We can't even find peas any more.' The anecdote speaks for itself.

I learnt to recognize selfishness in some and generosity in others, elegance of the heart and baseness of petty interests. I learnt that this had nothing to do with social class or geographic origin, but with the mysteries of the individual's psychological make-up. An infinity of kaleidoscopic figures. Same elements, different and changing configurations depending on the angle and the lighting of the moment.

Those were days of absence rather than presence. From then on, absence was what governed and structured my existence, twisted my mother's guts, hollowed out my grandmother's face month after month. By 1978, my father had been in prison for four years, with all the former members of Emperor Haile Selassie's government, waiting, hoping, pushing for a trial that we did not yet know, or want to admit, would never take place. Inside or outside, we were all captives waiting for a liberation that we wanted to believe was imminent.

My mother, overcome with loneliness, kept on hitting her head against the brick wall of a language she didn't understand and a universe that had become opaque and undecipherable. What was she to do? I saw her torn between her duty as a wife and mother, every day more distressed by the rumours, the contradictory news, the fear of losing everything, the fear of doing the wrong thing, the fear of not knowing what to do, the fear that something would happen to me on my way to school or on my way home, the fear that they would kill her husband like they'd killed so many others, the fear of searches, robbery and rape, the fear of not earning enough from her piano and French lessons to put food on the table, the fear of staying, the fear of leaving, of having to start all over in France at the age of fifty-two, without degrees and in poor health.

After attacking men, then women, the military took action against the young, forcibly conscripted, flung alive into prison or dead into the streets. Too many dead, too much violence, too much fear and no more hope. It was no longer a matter of waiting but of surviving. I was about to turn fourteen. I would no longer be considered the daughter of a French women and as an Ethiopian I'd be ripe for revolutionary service or prison. Leave? We would have to, no question about it, in a year, at the very most, my God! Another twelve months, like this? Between now and then, there'd be another Christmas, another Easter, another anniversary of the revolution. They always freed some prisoners for the occasion, maybe this time it would be his turn. So hold firm, stay a bit longer, what a pity it would be to miss him by so little, after all this time.

A sudden raid triggered our departure. This time, my mother thought the soldiers were searching for me. Five days later, we had left the country.

Fifth floor, door to the right. My mother, our valises and I jolted up in a tiny lift through the smell of wax for oak doors, the shine of copper door handles polished daily and the dense silence of the stairway carpeting.

The shrill sound of a doorbell, arms embracing me, the smell of my aunt's cologne and, through the crook of her elbow, the sky blue carpeting running from the entrance past the half-open living-room door to the screen of a TV set. In her blue velvet armchair, crocheted white antimacassars on its back and arms, sits my maternal grandmother. She's watching the game show *Des chiffres et des lettres*. I hadn't seen her for four years, ever since she gave me that Niçois folk costume and I posed next to her with the big matching doll I'd received for Christmas.

Grandmother gets up with difficulty like someone whose space has wedded the curve of the armchair. She smiles, happy and relieved to find us safe and sound. My aunt fusses, sees to our every need: 'Look how you've grown! How was the trip? Not too tired, Joe? Give that to me, I'll take care of it.' Words of no import but of great tenderness, shy and awkward, conveying so much love but sounding so far away. Same language, different planet. My mother cries. She lets go. Finally, she's back with her family, in her country. She will not have to fear for my life or her safety any more.

I look at them, not entirely there. Back in Ethiopia, my grand-mother Tato is sitting in her wooden armchair by the windows on her veranda. Tall, skinny and upright, she looks unseeing at the hundred-year-old pine trees in the courtyard. She waits. She prays. She hopes to see her son again. I will probably never see her again. Slam the door and make a clean break. Amputation rather than division.

On the dining-room buffet, the row of framed family photos has grown longer. The latest arrivals, those who've grown up, faces I don't know or recognize any more. My grandmother's two cats are no longer purring on the sofa. They died of old age last year. Aside from that, nothing has changed. Every object is exactly at the spot where my memory left it. My grandmother's box of mint candies on the sideboard near her armchair, the imitation-lace oil-cloth on the dining-room table, the crystal cordial glasses on the marble table, the tick-tock of my great-grandmother's pendulum on the commode in the entrance, the planters with geraniums on the balcony, the porcelain knickknacks on the radiator covers, and the painted wood birds inserted into the plant pots. Nothing has changed but everything seemed foreign to me.

My mother has stopped crying. Now she's talking non-stop, wringing her hands, pounding her chest, raising her eyes to the sky, tragic. Auntie Jeanne and Grandmother listen to her, fascinated, upset, horrified, distraught. They gasp, Grandmother nervously unwinds her rosary, they pour a little whiskey again, my mother changes her pose, I feel like throwing up. Screw my mother, her pain, her sighs, her crocodile tears and the photo of the Pope looking at us from his gold plastic frame. Fuck little Jesus, God the Father and his whole gang, none of whom answered my prayers; this revolution that delivered my mother, our valises and me in this month of April to the sorrow of exile; hope and its maybes and the it'll-be-all-right. Everything, yes everything, has become foreign to me.

Actually, it hasn't. I'm the one who's foreign. All the more so as I am here *chez moi*. Also.

Chez moi. At home. What an odd expression when you think about it! *Chez moi,* where? And me, who, or rather which me? Since there's necessarily one on the outside to say this, one who observes the other go in. One who has a general view of the inside and the outside, one who can only refer to herself as such in relationship to the other. Does this mean that one stays outside while the other thinks she's *chez elle?* Wouldn't that indicate something of a hiatus right from the start between two me's, two spaces, one that would correspond to the self as a being outside space-time and a me that would espouse this space-time entirely?

In which case, wouldn't *chez moi* indicate fluctuation rather than espousal? A dialogue between a here and an elsewhere within the universe? If we exist not 'in thin air' but in a body, of earth and of flesh, we couldn't live without the atmosphere we breathe thanks to the plant world. Our *chez moi* is wind. It carries the earth that we inhabit in the cycle of life and death. It's an intertwining of breaths and coexistences, a movement of absorption and dispersion. It journeys.

I exist as a human being in and by a cluster of interconnections. A dynamic that founds me and with which I interact in turn. Figure of the spiral, the DNA, also figure of the cross, as a junction of material horizontality and immaterial verticality. I'm an intersection. The task is to inhabit it knowingly, to be there, in other words, to realize that it's *chez moi*. Isn't this what is said, conveyed, transmitted from continent to continent, from island to island, from millennium to millennium, by songs, gestures and signs, myths, sacred texts and tales? This summons to realize, in both senses of the term (of becoming aware and of fulfilling) what we are: beings at the confluence of the spiritual and the material?

It almost always begins with a journey, a departure, often violent, always necessary, for this disjunction is the first condition of the story and of its quest. Interestingly, in French as in English, relating means connecting disjoined elements but also narrating a journey. Regardless of the transmutations, it has the selfsame destination: the return home, *chez soi*.

Thus, human beings forge themselves in relating but also in the story they create of this relation-journey. There is nothing human without specific languages (*langues*) and no specific languages (*langues*) without storytelling, since specific languages (*langues*) are from outset the saying of a being in the world. Yet, and this is what I mean by intersection, I don't only exist in and by a specific language (*langue*)—the horizontal plane—but also because I am traversed by language (*langage*, or language as universal category) which transcends all individual languages (*langues*) —the vertical plane. Without this language, the specific language would remain a dead letter. This is the case when we are disconnected from the point of intersection between *langue* and *langage*.

Let us now compare this *chez moi*, as expressed in French, with the way the idea is spoken of in another language. In Amharic, the *chez moi* doesn't exist by itself. It is always associated with a place or a feeling. 'Come *chez moi*' would be translated as 'Come into my house.' The 'I' that possesses is itself welcomed. In the order of enunciation, it is the element 'house' that comes first. The me comes after; it is appended to it. There's the house and the possessive particle after: *béten* / house-me. Even in the grammatical version where the me comes before the object, it is itself preceded by the 'ye' that indicates: *ye ené bet* / this me house. The 'me' is framed on both sides, so to speak. It isn't first. It exists in a perpetual interaction. It does not have primacy. Rather than being contingent on it, what surrounds and contains it exists in the relationships between them.

Paradoxically, it seems to me that the supremacy of the 'me' in the *chez moi* in French is more indicative of fragility than of power. A 'me' all alone is much more fragile than a 'me' with and in something. Its pre-eminence isolates it. The 'me' seems to rely on itself alone. It isn't included, it includes.

Nevertheless, the two grammatical structures join each other on a common interstice. The *moi*, as I was saying at the beginning, is not only me, it's also *chez*. There is an interval between the '*chez*' and the '*moi*' that presupposes and calls for a displacement. It is this passage to which we must be attentive. Because this is where the play of identification *and* of dis-identification is situated. Without this oscillation, the a priori fluid relation can freeze into univocality and become exclusive, and the displacement can harden into conquest of place. The espousal of *an* identity, religion and so on is what separates the individual from herself, Krishnamurti says in his *Talks with American Students*, and it engenders the divisions that provoke war.

This is so true, so simple, and so hard to assume in a society which is always urging us to be this *or* that, and which sees the interstice as a space to fill rather than a path to take.

III

The Blind Spot

The search depends on the seeker.

Osho

'Where are you from?'

'My mother's French and my father's Ethiopian.'

That's where it starts, with a question and a way of responding. The one conditioning the other and modifying it as you go along. Gradually, an implicit question emerges: Is the state of being *métis* a blind spot?

It used to amuse me considerably that no one in France can peg me to a specific identity. I would change countries as often as people change underwear, depending on the projections of my interlocutors: Iranian, Caribbean, Indian, Brazilian, Maghrebi, Fulani, Mauritanian, everything except Ethiopian and French, naturally. Why not? As a child, I had my Russian and then my Gypsy period, to the point of believing that my parents had kidnapped me . . . Is this what explains my reply, the first that would come to mind when I'd be asked where I come from, as if, by throwing onto my parents the weight of a designated origin, I left myself the possibility of going about my business somewhere else? Because in all this, I'm not there. The affiliation with a country, with an identity doesn't seem to concern me. You might say that it's unavoidable since there are two of them. Except that in my case, I'm not accumulating identities, I'm getting out of them. I'm leaving them to my parents. It may very well be clear and established that my mother is French and my father Ethiopian, but my own identity, on the other hand, remains undefined. That's not a stance or a desire on my part. That's simply how it is and it's not a subject of concern. The *métis* identity? I couldn't care less. It's not my problem and I can't even imagine that it could be. I know from my mother that I'm *métis*, meaning a child whose parents are from two different continents, and that's all. Which says nothing, since two continents are a bit too big and vague to refer to. As I understood it from my mother at the time, in Ethiopia, this word says nothing of the racial assumptions with which it is charged. It refers to geographic spaces rather than power relations between dominant and dominated cultures. The only assumption that I see in it is that of a hierarchy in the mix. Only the children of two different continents, according to my mother, could call themselves *métis*. The others, those from two countries, could not. What are they called? Nothing. There is no word for them. As a result, the expression *métis* is associated in my mind with a mix of the highest order. Two countries? Seriously? Pfah. I've got two continents going for me. That's another level altogether. All joking aside, if that's all there is to it, the word's too vague, too pompous and ultimately pretty hollow. My mother seems to like it, and even be proud of it, as if it were a trophy of sorts. For what, for whom? I don't really know. After all, that's her affair. What do I have to do with a useless term since it doesn't meet any personal need? Question of age and context. Children do not ask all these identity-related questions unless their environment and the grown-ups in their lives pressure them to do so. And when they do, the questions are much deeper than a matter of territory or administrative status. My origin or origins do not puzzle me and I don't recall anyone ever asking me about them in Ethiopia. I was, that's all. *Chez moi* was also not in doubt. For that to happen, you have to have been separated from it or have others invade it. But neither my native country nor my family were conquered. Ethiopia had experienced war and the Italian occupation for six years, but not colonization. The very notion is totally foreign to me and remains so for a long time after my arrival in France. It isn't until I'm about twenty-five that I begin to pay close attention to the subject, due to the problems I'm facing in the professional world and what that says of the society in which I live. Until then, colonization is something remote, belonging to the past. On the other hand, I feel directly concerned by the apartheid regime, the monstrosity of which obsesses me.

It is thus in France, separated from my familiar surroundings, that this *chez moi* and my mix become subject to questioning. Firstly internally, because of the feeling of disparity that I mentioned above, even within my French family. My impression is of coming not so much from a foreign country as from a different planet. How did the fact of being *métis* impact a feeling that any person in exile might experience? Is there even any need to move to a different country to feel this way? A few metres sometimes suffice, in any city in the world, from one district to another, and even often, on a much more reduced scale, simply crossing one's own street. Did my duality contribute to accentuating this impression of foreignness and even to anchoring it? Being a foreigner is an external status, or at least that's all there should be to it . . . It can afflict the individual depending on the circumstances that brought her to move and the place where she finds herself, but it can also comfort her when she feels foreign. The status legitimates the feeling, identifies it and explains it in factual terms. It is only natural, after all, to feel foreign when you are so by your country, your language and your culture. But how strange it is when none of these factors are there to justify it. The destiny of the *métis*, as common wisdom would have it, seeing the *métis* as forever limping between two shores, incapable of being wholly present on either? And what if it were exactly the opposite, namely, the incapacity to see the *métis* as a full-fledged being bringing the two together? History *oblige*, since the existence of being as a term in Western societies is indissociable from colonial violence. No matter what anyone says, it pervades the term *métis* and the route of the *métis*. But let's not get ahead of ourselves. At this point in my story, the period of my arrival in France and my adolescence, these questions do not yet concern me. It's important for me to stress this point, because people have such difficulty thinking of the state of being '*métis*' outside a whole series of negative and positive preconceptions attached to the term.

So when I arrive in France, I know I'm *métis* according to my mother's definition, but I don't define myself as such and no one bothers me about it. Not the professors and not the students. I'm first of all a teenager, a high-school student. The question of my origins comes up often, but that's all. I note in passing that we were in the eighties. There is nothing like the diversity of origins that exists today in the school environment. My first others, students from the eighteenth and nineteenth arrondissements, were not used to being around people from all over the world as were those from Addis Ababa. I must have stood out like an odd duck among them. That they ask me where I come from seems perfectly natural and is not a problem for me. On the contrary, I see it as a sign of curiosity and interest in me. In short, nothing to make a fuss about. It's a way of saying hello and starting a conversation that may or may not continue. Usually it comes to a quick end because I'm shy, but also especially because I don't share the same interests. I adore walking the streets of Paris, visiting museums, reading, and whenever I can, going to movies or to the theatre. None of which appeals to most of the others and so I do these things alone. I'm surprised to see that my classmates don't know and aren't even interested in their city and what it has to offer. Most of them stick to their neighbourhood, their parties, and playing flipper in the local cafe. They haven't been deprived of freedom as I was in Addis Ababa, and more importantly, they are not intending, as I already do, to embrace the life of an artist and social misfit. It isn't surprising therefore that my first friendships were made at the school theatre club with other oddballs who do not partake in the ordinary song and dance.

So here I am, growing up like everyone else, and completely overwhelmed by a body that has suddenly become too different from the others. Too fully developed, too conspicuous for my age. Too much. A woman's body that is a nuisance to me and attracts the gaze of men who see what I am not yet. A subject of concern and of danger for my mother, an image in the eyes of others who steal an identity from me that I haven't had the time to construct, with which I'm wrestling, at variance with my age and my entourage. I don't know what to do with myself. Ill at ease with this label of beautiful *métis* that's being thrown at me.

I thought of myself as the bearer of an elsewhere, a richness for those who'd never left the confines of France. I discover myself in the eyes of others and do not recognize what I see. The object of predation or of envy, the richness becomes a risk, that of an exotic fantasy. Where do you come from? The curiosity of the other high-school students is no longer as innocent and neither are my answers. Strictly speaking, nothing's changed, but I intentionally begin with my French mother, with what we have in common, to distance myself from any exotic claims. I no longer confine myself to answering: I listen and observe. Will they be capable of hearing that I'm double, from this land and from another, or will they, as I begin to find, turn the elsewhere into the central, exclusive subject of conversation, the only one that I'll be expected to discuss, all because they have nothing to say to me? Could these French people who ask me so many things about Ethiopia, answer about France a fraction of the questions they are putting to me? Could they really forget to such an extent that they are dealing with a person, not a tourist brochure? And what exactly do they want to know? Why should my foreign ancestry be explained in terms of a country as a whole, and not in the private terms of French ancestry? Don't my father and mother have the right to their own private story, and me, to mine?

Nothing doing. Ethiopia takes over, takes up all the room. It is the central subject. I find myself almost having to excuse myself for being only half Ethiopian . . .

So I reverse the order of my answer and end up undermining its integrity: my father is Ethiopian and that should suffice. But it doesn't. This time it's my skin, its colour that creates a doubt. I'm not Black enough to be African. My compatriots are decidedly rather strange. Pronounced Ethiopian when I say my mother is French, here I am a questionable African by my father, all this for a matter of colorimetry.

Métis? All things considered, why not? Well, because it's not where I'm at, fortunately I have a life elsewhere, with people I love who can do without racial definitions. These remarks concern the French in general who do not ask themselves questions about the questions they ask, and especially those in the art world. I end up saying I'm *métis*, because I have to say something in this country, without adding technical details, just to see. And I do see, all too quickly. I am a blind spot.

This blind spot was the starting point of my interest in the state known as *métis*. Not for how people saw my insignificant self but for what, through me, they could not seem to accept. One could not help but notice a contradiction between the need to define me—I'm restricting myself to the world of show business—the seeming clarity of the designation '*métis*' and the incapacity to understand it. Why reproach me for not being Black enough for an African—no one ever reproached me for not being white enough for a Frenchwoman—knowing that I was *métis*, and therefore, according to the same logic, also European? What's wrong with this picture? as Van Morrison asks in his song. Something like a blind spot that now requires closer scrutiny.

The expression blind spot, *point aveugle* in French, is used in the humanities to designate an 'unthought', a hidden, invisible subject or angle of a subject that needs to be examined. The blind spot in this context serves as a focus on a question left in the shadows. Oddly, although the French term is used often, that particular sense of the expression is not found in French dictionaries. I must admit that this disturbed me at first and then amused me. A blind spot in the dictionary: that's something worth paying attention to. After all, isn't it as its name indicates something we don't see?

What interests me here is to question not so much the blind spot as the source of the blindness. The common expression focuses on what's not seen, thereby externalizing a phenomenon that is first and foremost internal, as is clear from the definition of the term in optics. Here is the definition in the Oxford Dictionary, for instance: 'the spot on the retina which is insensible to light', further developed in Wikipedia: 'Because there are no cells to detect light on the optic disc, the corresponding part of the field of vision is invisible.'

The blind spot, in this sense, is not a mere metaphor that would enable me to refer to or introduce a subject, in this case the state of being *métis*, thereby implying that it has not been the subject of study—which is by no means the case—but, rather, a guide for thinking about it. Who's the observer and who's the observed? What is it that the observer doesn't see? A spot in the other, the other as a whole, or the observer's own way of seeing? Where are they situated in relation to each other? In a linear, frontal, static relationship, in which it is always the same one who observes and the same one who's observed with no possibility of moving them? Wouldn't this be the effect of an additional optical illusion, preventing us from seeing both the observer and the observed in their common, complementary relationship, making the observer an observed and the observed, an observer? From where do they look at each other? If the spot on the retina that does not see is fixed, the spot on the visual field depending on where one is.

It is not a question of answering these impenetrable questions, I do not pretend to do so and that's not the point, but simply to consider, through this idea of the blind spot, other ways of looking at this state of being *métis*. And thus to shift away from the centre from which it is most often approached, namely, that of colonial violence. To argue that there are historic reasons for this is to limit oneself to the point of view of the West alone. The *métis* state turns round in circles at this same centre. Whether it is to counter it or to magnify it does not change a thing. I've been struck by how few alternatives have been proposed. Either it is thought of within this violence or, to get out of it, it is dissolved into an abstraction, a theoretical speculation, such as this concept of *métissage* which, as beautiful and interesting as it may be, has little to do with the fact of being *métis*. I have to admit I'm rather wary of this concept, which tells us more about those who conceived it, who, for the most part, are not *métis* themselves, and remains dependent on a compartmentalized view of the world. A question of words or state of mind? Mightn't the very term *métis* be the source of the problem, condemning us to see the *métis* only through the conditions that forged the word?

To return to my story, the realization of what people cannot conceive and that seems obvious to me—a person of Ethiopian *and* French ancestry—is what makes me suspicious of the term. It's true that I haven't closely examined what it corresponds to, but then again, why would I have? I'm a person, not a word. *Métis* is neither my name nor my nationality, just a label used to classify me as mixed. More than the designation itself, it's the quasi-obsessive need for classification that troubles me in the theatre world. In the political or scientific field, I suppose I could perhaps understand it. But it seems unnatural in the world of fiction. Well, so be it. I have to deal with it. But with what precisely, given that I don't seem to meet the requirements of the *métis* label either? What then is *métis* the name of?

To begin with, *métis* is an adjective not a noun, derived from the Latin *mestiz, mixtus*, meaning 'mixture'. *Métis*, according to the dictionary *Robert*, is what is mixed, 'made half of one thing and half of another'. The adjective will thereafter be reserved to the textile sector. One speaks of *métis* cloth or linen. And so my understanding of the term is obsolete and could therefore explain the recurrent misunderstandings in castings. I would present myself as a derivative version of this original use—my parents being neither fabric nor things—only to discover that this sense of the term was outdated. If *métis* no longer refers to a mix, what would be the contemporary definition? The answer is blood curdling: '1615, *Métice*, from Portuguese, a person from a crossbreeding of races; a cross between different varieties of a single species.' This time, it is not outdated, incomprehensible or rare. This is the second and last entry for the word *métis*. There is no third that would leave hope for a way out. We are smack in the midst of the transatlantic deportation and everything continues as it was: the abjectness of race, the 'cross-breeding' that supplants the fluidity of the mix with the coldness of zoological experimentation, the mechanism of racial classification and its offshoots—mulatto, Eurasian, quadroon. *Métis* has changed status. From an adjective, it has become a noun. It no longer describes a person, it is the person, which amounts to removing or replacing the person. The *métis* as such does not exist, all that exists is the product of crossbred races. An excretion of the racial manufacture. I might add to this picture that whereas a person cannot have an antonym, the *métis* can and does: 'pure'. Strict grammatical logic . . .

I pursue my investigation and look into the charms of the term 'crossbreeding', with particular appreciation for the examples given in biology: 'Hybridization; crossbreeding. Improving a breed of cattle by crossbreeding.' Knowing that crossbreeding is a 'method of reproduction by fertilization carried out selectively between individuals, animals or plants of a single species or related species', what exactly would this 'crossbreeding of races' mean with regard to me? Would I be an improved cow?

If I understand correctly, the '*métis*' offspring, as a product of this crossbreeding, would derive from an intention, a calculation, from scientists fiddling around, but certainly not from a consensual encounter. And between humans, that's called rape. Isn't it? No need to go searching through history books, just open a dictionary. *Robert*, the newly revised edition, corrected and updated in 1990. The year I look up the exact definition of the word *métis*. In comparison, the dictionary definition of race seems inoffensive. It doesn't prejudge the abject use that will be made of it, unlike that of the *métis*, the violence of which is intrinsic. In fact, it is through the notion of *métis* that 'purity of race' is introduced. With it that this race, which is a family affair at the outset, becomes pathologically racial and racist.

Oddly, whereas the term race prompts cries of outrage, and even demands that it be suppressed, not a whole lot of people seem bothered by the term *métis*, though it embodies the folly of racial division. Could this be a matter of hiding the crime weapon? Sorry for the cosmetic arrangements and flights of lyricism around the word. It's not the joyful mix of peoples and the harmony of cultures to which it attests, but first and foremost to racial segregation. The laboratory that initiated the 'crossbreeding of races' has its foundations in the holds of the ships of the transatlantic deportation.

Times have changed, one might argue. *Métis* doesn't have the same resonance today as it did in the seventeenth century, at the height of the colonial period. Really?

The ninth edition of the dictionary of the French Academy, the third and final volume of which was published in 2011, defines it as follows: '*Métis* refers to a person whose parents are of different races: *métis* children, a *métis* woman. Noun: a métis (m), a *métisse* (f).'

Now, that's a fine development by way of omission rather than transformation. The colonial and racist reference has disappeared between the eighth and the ninth edition, but not the reference to race. The 1932–35 version reads as follows: 'a person born of parents from different races, especially, from a white man and a coloured woman, or a coloured man and a white woman. *Natural Spaniards and métis Spaniards. A métis woman.* Also refers to animals that are engendered from two species.'

I thought it useful to quote this in its entirety to gain a better grasp of what is still at work in people's minds. Because the *métis* is still seen in terms of colour. The good or bad conscience, depending on the angle, of racial segregation. The *métis*, in the French imagination, the one that no one knows where to put in audiovisual fiction, is this one, the mulatto. When it's not noticeable in terms of skin colour and hair, everything's all right. A little touch of the exotic, like salt enhancing the flavour of a dish, is always welcome. As long as the dominant colour is white and the hair is gently wavy. In that case, you won't be called *métis*, you'll be French, like Isabelle Adjani. To put it plainly, the *métis* as such, disturbing as it does the fine colorimetric order of races, is requested to disappear and to blend in on one side or the other of the fence. In France it remains an affair between whites and Blacks, managed by whites alone. In the audiovisual field and in the French colonial imaginary, this is understood. I'll leave it at that.

This ninth edition of the dictionary of the French Academy seems to open broader perspectives. The *métis* is no longer confined to two colours and to the colonial relationship alone. That said, it remains subordinate to race. Like the minds of the academicians. In both editions, not only do races crossbreed or are crossbred but so do people of different races. The *métis* has a right to parents and is thereby made more human in a sense. Fine, but can anyone explain to me what parents of different races are when at the same time we know that the notion of race is scientifically unfounded? Logically, this statement offers one alternative only: either the *métis* does not exist, because the very ground on which the concept stands—racial difference—does not exist, or, insofar as race is maintained and embedded at the core of the identity, it exists only as an ideological posture. We can see here an attempt to square the circle. Impossible to get rid of race without renouncing the term *métis*. You can't have one without the other. Once more, it is clearly to racial division not to mixture that the term refers.

Let us now look at what this same revised and corrected edition has to say about race. It's fascinating to see the convoluted paths the editors take to come out with their hands clean: 'Each of the major groups into which the human species is divided superficially, based on distinctive physical traits that have remained constant or have appeared, due to geographical isolation for prolonged periods. A man of Black race, of white race, of yellow race. The mix, the crossbreeding of races. The term is inappropriately used to refer to an ethnic group.' I can't help thinking of the French stand-up comic Coluche's line about technocrats: 'Technocrats are guys who, by the time they've finished answering your question, make you wonder what you asked them in the first place!' What's this business about geographic isolation for 'prolonged periods'? Human beings have been moving around for a rather 'prolonged' period, haven't they? This definition reminds me of a cooking recipe: let it sit for a prolonged period in an isolated corner and, poof, depending on which way your kitchen is facing, you'll come out with a yellow, a Black or, who knows, a red whatever. You have been warned: avoid staying isolated in one place for a 'prolonged period', you never know what can remain constant or appear.

The *Larousse* has the virtue, at least, of being more explicit: 'Category of classification of the human species according to morphological or cultural criteria, without any scientific basis, the use of which underpins various racist forms and practices. Faced with human diversity, a classification based on the most immediately apparent criteria—especially skin colour—was established and prevailed throughout the nineteenth century. Advances in genetics have led to a rejection of all attempts at racial classification for humans.'

In this sense, the *métis*, appended as it is to race, cannot exist. It's a figment of the imagination, a creature born of the lucubrations of a band of psychopathic classifiers. So now, it is no longer a question of races but of ethnic origin. '*Métis* is someone born from the union of two people of different ethnic origin.'

Here I am, a so-called *métis*, feeling lost. Scholars do not at all agree on their definitions. Whereas the *Larousse* 'saves' the term *métis* by detaching it from race and entrusting it to ethnicity, the French Academy stresses the impossible slippage from one to the other. And this is perfectly understandable. Since *métis* would have nothing to do with ethnicity either.

One must say that, given the definition of the term ethnicity according to the *Larousse*—'A human group with a homogenous economic, social and family structure, whose unity is based on a community of language, culture and group consciousness'—a great many people of the same 'race' could consider themselves *métis*. A real catch-all term in the end. Either you lose you *métis*-ness, or you keep it nice and fresh in the racial fads department.

Ultimately, *métis* can only be the name of a racial ideology, including in the new definition given in the *Larousse*. The vocabulary has changed, to be sure, but it is haunted by the same ghosts. Even if they show themselves in a more pleasant light, their monstrosity persists. The lexical variants of the term do not transform the conditions of its manufacture. Shifting from racial difference to ethnic difference does not remove us from a model of classification governed by a desire for domination. Who cares to classify people from 'ethnicities' of the same colour as *métis*, which would come down to putting them on the same level as others? Here again, racial hierarchy seems to have shifted to that of ethnicity, since it has to be said that there are some who are more ethnic than others, and the rules of distribution on this point have not changed ... The apparent neutrality of the definition proceeds from thought patterns that are not neutral at all.

Can the blood of a word be washed off? Act as if the ignominy of its manufacture were not oozing from the pages of dictionaries? Why hold onto it? Considering its history, it can't be said that it is nicer or less *racist* than negro, coon, chink, and other foul expressions. So what are we holding on to and more precisely, what do we not want to let go of? Would it be a reading of the human species positing race, with all it implies of supposed fixity and 'purity', as primary? Regardless of the good intentions, I don't see how we can break free of the aporia of race using such a term. On the contrary, in fact, it can only draw us further in by creating a new one, equally delusory and all the more pernicious.

How then to designate people with plural origins? It all depends on the story you want to tell. Going from *métis* to whatchamacallit won't resolve a thing. A *métis* people in general does not exist, except as a Western invention. Replacing the word will not be a game changer if the narrative is not changed. Dethroning it would be a step in the right direction. Bringing the term back to its original status as an adjective, for weaving and interweaving. And putting † before the use of *métis* for humans to indicate that this meaning is obsolete. No need for lexical battles to achieve this; only the ability to dream. The dream of opening a dictionary and the *métis* entry reading as follows: Used at the time of the division of the human species into races to refer to individuals resulting from a cross of races. Only the adjective *métis* is in use today. Not to be confused with *métissage* which served, in absurd times, to name a by-product of capitalist consumption.

It is important to stress that, outside the Western world, which covers quite an area, the word is untranslatable. It simply does not exist or else only as a Western import, attached to a colonial history and context. *Mestizo,* in Ethiopia, clearly reflects the Italian occupation and, at any rate, is never used any more; *hāfu,* in Japan, a loanword from the English word *half,* emerged in the 1970s. And these are just two examples. Does this mean that people, before Western domination, did not mix, or are we dealing with another relationship to difference?

The concept of *métis* as a racial marker is inherently connected to the West. I may be pushing at open doors, but I see that people are neglecting to walk through them. We are so conditioned by the racial paradigm that we forget that it is only one narrative among others. All peoples have invented themselves out of stories they chose to tell in order to exist in the world. Thousands of years went by before a tiny portion of them came up with the notion of race and its theories, and it remains foreign to a lot of cultures, even those that have been confronted with it. Seeing oneself as Gondaré, Igbo or Guarani, for instance, does not mean defining oneself by a racialized colour but, rather, in terms of a specific culture. The racial narrative is not a fatality. This by no means diminishes the atrocities that this invention causes still today and the need to counter it for a simple vital question. Neither am I saying that it's a mere fiction that we can allow ourselves to ignore, as if it weren't central, as if it didn't kill for real every day. No, what I'm questioning, with this *métis* as a starting point, is our submission to this narrative, as if it were the only one possible, and especially as if it wasn't a narrative? An obedience that traps us in the vicious circle of perpetrator and victim, dominator and dominated, option a *or* b, and condemns us to keep harping on the *same* story again and again. Postcolonial, decolonization, post, pre or neo, the reference is the same, central, unchanging, overriding. What we need now is not so much to replace one narrative with another, to value what has been depreciated, in a word to turn around, but, rather, to shift our position. Towards what, in all this, appears to be a blind spot: us, qua I, and what there is in common with the other. So I repeat my question: Is it possible to designate people with plural origins by a generic name, without lapsing into the disembodiment of race, in the sense that it strips the person of her body as of her landscapes?

To come back to the context in which this word started to perplex me, that of the performance milieu, at first *métis* signified the inability to conceive of the mix. It then became the door through which I entered the colonial past of France, then the West. Reading about this history enabled me to decipher the codes of representation with which I was confronted in my professional life, to understand the pathological nit-picking concerning skin colour, the obsession with classifying actors as racial types, but I still had a hard time understanding the hypocritical use of the term *métis*, given that it was always a matter of looking one hundred per cent of this or that origin. And I don't think that's changed much. The *métis* always remains someone that no one knows where to place, a thorn in the proper functioning of racial division, to which it evidently refers. Its absence from the controversies in contemporary France on the place of Afro-descendent actors is telling in this regard. It points to the self-same blind spot: the person. We have still not entered into a conversation between human beings. In my opinion, what we are latching onto in refusing to let go of the term *métis* is first and foremost racial segmentation. Witness the way in which the word 'parts' comes up again and again in this regard. Parts are distinct from one another. I've never accepted and continue to reject this dubious image in black and white that would make of me two slices of cake taped together.

I ended up seeing the term as a decoy to avoid pronouncing in France the word mulatto, to which it is related, and to perpetuate a colonial paradigm under a slightly more presentable mask. The world of representations, where the imaginaries and the image of a society are made, bears responsibility for this. In this context, therefore, if the point is to name the twofold origin, one could hardly say it's been a resounding success. To be a *métis* is rather like being confined to a no-man's-land. The hybridity that this milieu pretends to celebrate, become intolerable when they are actually confronted with it directly. Too complicated. And what for anyway?

I was struck in this by the difference in the perception of me as a *métis* in my two countries. In Ethiopia, my common filiation prevails over the foreigner, it swallows it. My hybridity is not a subject, no one cares, it's my business. All that matters is that I speak the language and espouse the lifestyle. That I'm also French does not contradict or conflict with the fact that I'm Ethiopian. My identity is not racial, it is a matter of family and culture. Does this mean that I'm complaining about not being regarded, conversely, as French in France? Not at all. That's neither my point nor my concern. I find it amusing to note that, between my two countries, which are equally arrogant, one seems more confident than the other. Ethiopia digests while France hiccups. I wonder, could the racial division make whoever clings to it paranoid?

In France, the *métis* is a kind of border post, embodying the dividing line between us and them in a more policed way. The one that serves as an observation point on the other, without having to go there. An image in general. A *métis* of Europe and Africa? You'll be an African in general. Of Europe and Asia? An Asian in general.

Here are two anecdotes on this subject, nearly thirty years apart.

The earlier one: The director of a TV movie is won over by my audition, but. There's a problem, a big one, the colour of my skin. Not Black enough to be credible as the wife of a high African government official, so super-Black of course. A geopolitical matter? No, just a question of looking African since that's what I'm supposed to be, so super-Black of course. Let's not go into unpleasant details, like pointing out that the so-called black colour of the people of this so-called Black Africa actually ranges from yellow ochre to midnight blue and all the pigments of brown and red ochre in-between. No. Let's keep it simple, practical, rational—in a word, French. Africa is a country with black Blacks who speak dialects in the midst of wild animals. Okay, so there are a few cities, thanks to colonization (idiotic but still tenacious in the minds of some people). So I stayed practical and declared that I could darken my skin. Appointment is made for verification after the prescribed UV sessions that I never did. So here I was again with the director, slightly browner from a light touch of self-tanner. Doubt in his eyes.

—Did you do the UV sessions?

—Absolutely. As you can see, I'm much darker now.

That was enough. He clearly saw that nothing much had changed, but the good man was reassured. The idea that I was almost Black was good enough for him. Everything fell back into place. Fortunately, there was Chester Himes to laugh about it, for such situations called to mind the mechanisms of racial segregation in the United States, where one drop of Black blood sufficed to make you Black. With a major difference, that in France, it wasn't a matter of saving my skin but of having a colour that corresponded to my classification. Incidentally, I would have liked to, out of personal taste, and also to look like something rather than like nothing as was increasingly my impression. That said, there is no reason to think it would have made things better. As this anecdote shows, it isn't so much about colour as about a mental projection.

Now for the more recent anecdote. High level, theatre. She reads, thinks, is engaged, signs petitions for refugees, she is a sophisticated Frenchwoman, open-minded, with a heart, a brain and the proper skin colour, meaning white. She thinks you're an extraordinary actor and that you should play the role of Othello because: 'Wouldn't it be great to have a Black woman playing

Othello?' You say nothing, nothing more to say, tired, you just report this new status of Black serving the white feminist cause to your daughters, who burst out laughing: 'What? But you're not even Black. Right?'

Sure, it would be funny, if it wasn't enough to make you cry. This impairment in the perception of the other. For what she is, not for what one has decided, supposed, fantasized that she should be. Six hundred years that we've been interacting, willy-nilly, for better or for worse, and nothing. People continue to refer to others by their colour in general, never by their names, as if they didn't have any, as if they didn't have a language that gave them meaning. Not long ago, a slogan proclaimed: 'We are all strangers, Italian, Portuguese, Turk, Spaniard, Armenian . . . Black.' Some have the right to a country, while the others—Cameroonian, Malian, Beninese, Senegalese, Congolese, Togolese, Mauritanians, Haitians, Guyanese, Guadeloupian, Reunionese . . . were simply Black, as usual. Ignorance or intellectual laziness? Are people never tired of being so thoroughly white?

Today, many years after my first experiences as a *métis* actor, I wonder what is the use of this term if not to feed fantasies about the other whom one doesn't make the effort to encounter. What good is the term *métis* in general, when, despite the current good intentions, it merely stresses a specific Eurocentric history?

In any case, I do not recognize myself in it. This story is not mine, and the term is too narrow to contain the person I am.

Ainoko, child of encounter, they used to say in Japanese, a term that finds its way in other forms with other sonorities in so many places. It reminds me of my mother's version with her continents. It speaks of a journey, a crossing, the path of two beings towards each other, landscapes of love. A story. Where I come from.

IV

The Starting Point

*We do not belong to a country, Grace said, we do not belong to
any country made by the hand of man. We belong to the moon
that makes the tides and the menses. The ocean's heritage lasts
longer than a country's. We do not belong to history, we belong
to the cycles of the invisible placenta.*

Kossi Efoui, *Cantique de l'acacia*

This story begins with an emperor and an architect. The year is
1948, and we're in the period of postwar reconstruction. The
International Union of Architects organizes a competition for the
new imperial palace of Emperor Haile Selassie with financial support
from UNESCO. Among the 113 participating architects and engi-
neers is a young Frenchman, Henri Chomette, who works in the
north of France. This is his first contact with Africa and a turning
point in his career, as it will soon be in the destiny of my future
mother, Josée Roumieu. Shortly after the competition in which he
ranked second, Henri moves to Addis Ababa and chooses to work
in Africa deeming French architecture poisoned by what he terms

'the dictatorship of calculations over art, regulations over spirit, numbers over the heart.' He opens his first Bureau d'Études Henri Chomette (BEHC) in West Africa and will go on to become one of the most prominent architects of sub-Saharan Africa during Les Trente Glorieuses.[6] Through these regional offices, he proposes a practice and philosophy of architecture more in sync with the culture, geography and materials of each country than those parachuted into Africa from offices in colonial France. No doubt this is what will earn him the attention and trust of the emperor who, in 1953, appoints Henri Chomette architect and urban planner of the city of Addis Ababa.

That same year, the man who will become my father, Mammo Tadessé, returns home after nine years studying in Cairo and Paris. He's twenty-nine years old, his pockets full of diplomas, and he plans to set up his own business. Destiny—in this case, the will of the emperor—will decide otherwise. The Italian occupation had decimated a generation of intellectuals and obstructed the emergence of a new one. For its reconstruction, the empire needs young people like Mammo who've been educated abroad. Reluctant at first to join the civil service, he eventually lets himself be persuaded, finding it ultimately more exhilarating to contribute to the development of the country than to work for more self-centred ends, and so begins his career in the Ministry of Foreign Trade.

Five thousand kilometres away, Josée in Paris has also just found a position in the Ministry of Foreign Trade, but for her it is only to pay the bills. What she's passionate about, what she lives

---

6 Léo Noyer Dupleix, 'Henri Chomette et l'architecture des lieux de pouvoir en Afrique subsaharienne,' *In Situ* 34 (2018): 1–44.

for is music. She would have liked to be a pianist, but neither her health nor the narrowmindedness of her family allowed her to do so. Newly arrived from Béziers, a small town in the south of France, she does what she can to survive in the capital, and most of her earnings go to paying doctors incapable of curing the mysterious illness that is devouring her stomach. By the time she meets Henri at the ministry—he is often there on business—this woman of great beauty with a thirst for other horizons has already had many extravagant adventures in Egypt and Lebanon, where she narrowly escaped confinement in harems, as the friendly invitations of visiting entrepreneurs turned out to have less unselfish aims than they pretended. Henri and Josée become friends, then lovers. It is at his invitation that she travels to Ethiopia for the first time.

Nineteen fifty-five. Addis Ababa is preparing for the silver jubilee of the emperor's reign. The Chomette team revamps a movie theatre constructed by the Italians to accommodate cultural events and, firstly, the jubilee festivities. Henri has Josée join the team in charge of decoration, and she lands in Addis with the red velvet material intended for the stage curtain. At the jubilee party, Josée meets a young French-speaking Ethiopian deputy minister, Mammo. A few days later she returns to Paris and the story could have ended there. Josée was set to marry Henri, at least that's what both of them were hoping to do once he is cured of his demons. For Henri is homosexual, which at the time means he's sick. Three years go by and nothing has changed, of course. Josée's health and morale deteriorate and she finally resolves to turn the page. Leave Henri, leave France, leave in search of light, of meaning, of an elsewhere that would wrest her from her physical sufferings. Her decision is made, she will go to India, to the Sri Aurobindo ashram.

Thinking she's too fragile for the trip, Henri urges her to make a stopover in Ethiopia. There she will be welcomed by friends and can regain some strength before the big jump.

Second trip to Ethiopia, three years after the evening when Josée first set eyes on the man who will become my father. She isn't planning to stay, of course, just looking to escape her suffering body. For the time being, Ethiopia is just a sunny resort on the way to India.

Henri's friends who welcome her on her arrival introduce her to an Italian doctor who will finally diagnose the ailment that has been plaguing her and that none of the many bigwigs consulted in Paris were able to figure out: a commonplace appendicitis. She has to be operated on right away. She is sent to a town 353 kilometres from Addis, where the streets and squares stretch out in the shade of carob, flamboyant and jacaranda trees. A highly regarded French surgeon has been practising there for a while, and not just any surgeon since he's Vincent Auriol's former personal physician. He is said to have fallen into disgrace as a result of a mysterious Freemason conspiracy that blamed him for a shady affair of theft he did not commit. His medical licence was revoked in France following this accusation and he moved to Dire Dawa, a pleasant town, founded during the building of the Franco-Ethiopian Railway connecting Djibouti to Addis Ababa, and where a sizeable French community had settled as a result.

Josée sees a sign of destiny in this incredible chain of circumstances. She has never been so surrounded and well cared for as in this distant land that brings her closer to her compatriots and restores the hope she'd abandoned of being cured.

The routine operation will turn into a vision of horror, as the infection, ignored for too long, has devoured her lower stomach. The pariah surgeon decides to leave an ovary instead of removing both, out of concern for a young woman who has not yet had a child. A new period begins, one of convalescence in the shade of the bougainvillaeas in her hosts' garden that gradually eclipses the call of India, which was perhaps in the end but the gateway to this fleeting encounter during the jubilee.

His voice. At a casual gathering one evening, in the next room, she recognizes it instantly. She walks through the door. They will never leave each other again. Mammo takes Josée on a journey through the landscapes of his land. With him, she writes to her sister, her sufferings subside; by his side, she smiles.

Mammo introduces her to his mother. The understanding between them is immediate. A complicity of wounded women, which has no need for words and which they do not yet comprehend. This mother's eyes wish her the tenderness that she herself never received, neither from a father, nor from a husband, nor from this body forced to give birth too young. Abducted at fourteen by her future husband with her family's blessings, a mother at fifteen, a widow at twenty-five, this tall noble woman gave up on everything except the happiness of her son. Belaynesh, Tato, my grandmother. She will be my mother's mother from Ethiopia, as she will be mine later. She asks her nothing, no explanations, no proofs, no statement of identity. One look at her son and she knows that Josée is the one he's chosen. She opens her arms to her. Ethiopia is no longer just the beautiful backdrop for Josée's love life, it is a house where she can take her place.

From intention to deed, the step isn't easy to take. When they are about to cross the threshold, both of them take fright. As their love assumes concrete shape, it awakens the demons of memory. They are no longer sheltered in the enchanted invisibility of Sundays in the countryside and evenings alone together. Outside, all the other days lie in wait, watching, lurking and reminding them that they are not alone, neither within nor without.

Mammo is a public figure; his private life is not his alone. How will they take this marriage to a foreigner by a member of the post-war Ethiopian government, who fought hard to maintain the country's independence? Is she more worthy than the princess to whom he has just been betrothed? Is this a way of valuing his country? The lover is first and foremost a subject of the emperor. He is not free to marry without the emperor's permission. Josée now realizes, as we see in the letters she wrote to her sister, that she is in Africa, that her heart's chosen one is Black and that she therefore is white. Mammo is no longer the man by whose side her heart smiles; he's an Ethiopian and she's French. The prospect of marriage entangles her in the threads of what had been until then only a backdrop: a country with its history, its language, its rules, the personality of its inhabitants. She is stricken with dread. In the fabric of her tapestry, never ever were threads of different colours to be interwoven.

She finds herself catapulted into the heart of a maelstrom of ancestral fears and prejudices. She discovers the racism of the people around her, of 'her' people. Has she spurned the advances of white men of 'quality' for a negro?! Disgusted, she quits her job at the French Embassy, stops seeing her circle of expatriates. But inside she's filled with fear. Could transgressing a boundary between races that centuries had obstinately separated and classified bring a curse down upon her? Forbidden love could only spawn monsters, vile and ridiculous 'chequered children', as she wrote, forever marked in her imagination with the seal of the impossible and unthinkable mix.

As the unofficially official fiancée of a statesman, she can no longer take a step without putting his reputation in jeopardy. Neither single nor married, she loses the freedom of the former without gaining the security of the latter. Mammo, in the meantime, does not seem to be in any hurry to marry her. Does he fear the emperor's refusal, and being forced to choose between a country and a woman? That their love will not withstand the inescapable differences of culture and mentality? That Josée will not succeed in adjusting to an Ethiopian society where he himself, because of his long stay abroad, often feels out of place? Was it because she's no longer simply Josée, but the fiancée of, that Mammo, in turn, vacillates?

What do they mean to each other? The desire of an elsewhere? The dream of security and power for a woman who was harassed from childhood? The dream for him of a woman unbound by stifling conventions, whose spirit restores the flavour of his lost freedom? She, so French, he, so Ethiopian, each one at loggerheads with their respective countries. They will always lack something, here or there. Between them, the aspiration to a completeness that comes up against the reality of their limits. After all, isn't what separates us from others the dream we have of them?

Perhaps with real obstacles, they would have been less likely to have these delusional fears. For nothing, nothing at all, actually stands in the way of their union. Josée's family are enthralled by the statesman, the man who finally seems to fulfil her desires. In Mammo's family, not a single voice is raised against them, far from it. Not even the voice of the emperor who, when Mammo at last decides to ask his permission to marry the foreigner, responds 'of course' without a moment's hesitation. No, what keeps them apart is not two continents but their apprehension of a new life.

Weeks go by, then months, then two years. Mammo still hesitates, and Josée finally decides to stop waiting for him and returns to the grey solitude of her Parisian life. Looking down from her window, she thinks of the child she will likely never have. She is thirty-five and has spent too many years hoping for an unattainable marriage. However, Mammo does not give up. Letter after letter, he calls her, beseeches her, desires her. Two years of obstinate beseeching. Is it her resistance or his own that he seeks to break?

What a strange arithmetic of evasions their story is! Destined to one another almost in spite of themselves.

Finally, she returns. For that smile.

Mammo begins vacillating again. Josée is furious, he plays for time, I come along.

My arrival is a complete surprise. I am the unexpected child they no longer dared dream of because of my mother's health, and probably also because of their fears. A gift that offers the legitimacy they dared not grant their love.

My mother will later speak to me of her pregnancy as an enchanted parenthesis. The only period without suffering. Busy with making this small being inside her, this body that has tormented her since she was eleven finally leaves her in peace. She dreams of a little boy. Not a girl, especially not. It's too hard to be a woman in this world. Power, strength, health, freedom, all belong to men. She will have her revenge through a male child. He won't be harassed, he won't have damned ovaries and he will at least have the advantage of being a man in a world ruled by white males, he who will be *métis*, a 'chequered' child. She has a name for him, Michael, like Saint Michael the Archangel, prince of the archangels, who proclaims the gospel, and slays the dragon. Oh please, God, let him be healthy!

She doesn't get all she wished for but at least I'm in good health. She is more than satisfied with that, in fact she is all too happy to have given birth to a normal child. End of the enchanted parenthesis. As soon as the placenta is expelled, her problems return. Haemorrhaging, transfusion, hepatitis. To prevent contamination, the doctors separate us. She will see me only from afar. The quarantine will last three months. I gain two additional mothers: Tato, my grandmother, and Feleketch, my nanny. My mother is haunted by the fear of being dispossessed of her child. It is out of the question for her to share me, as my father suggests, 'That's how things are done here,' he explains. 'It's not necessary that the biological mother be the one to raise the child. My mother has adopted her and she'd be very happy to keep her.' No. I'm the victory of her suffering body, her joy, her anchor.

***

The brilliant, thoughtful lover of the early days has become a nervous, anxious husband, who throws himself body and soul into his work, or rather into his calling. He has just been appointed Minister of Justice. Everything remains to be done, to be reformed, a whole system of often confusing not to say non-existent rules, incapable of meeting the needs of a changing society, is on the brink of paralysis and needs to be entirely overhauled. He is passionate about his mission. It devours him, invades all the space of their couple. Yet Josée supports him, listens to him, encourages him. He could have been content to deal with injustice, nobody was asking him to do so much, quite the contrary. But Mammo is neither a politician nor an obedient civil servant. He didn't seek power and doesn't care about it. Devoted to the cause of a progressive Ethiopia, he knows no laws other than those dictated by his intellectual integrity. My mother is proud to be at the side of this brilliant man, driven by an ideal that draws him into the exhilarating adventure of building a country.

She too would like to do something, to make herself useful, but she's not quite sure how. He wants none of her Christian charity. He sees it as an insult, an attack on the dignity of his people. 'Shut up, you don't understand anything, you know nothing about the mentality of this country, you're applying the mindset of a self-righteous Westerner who sees herself as superior to others. Do you think we've been waiting for you? You all have this way of reducing others to beggars. . . . What do you know about their history, about what they really need? You can't even speak the language.' But learning this language is precisely what she wants to do, now that she's sure she will stay, but god how difficult it is! After a few lessons, Josée gives up, discouraged. Mammo makes fun of the way she clumsily pronounces the few words she's learnt, she'll never succeed, and what's the point anyway? The rudiments of Amharic that she already has should suffice for her purposes, to give instructions to the servants, to go to the market, and joke around a bit with Tato. Otherwise, all the people around her speak French or English. She'd like to speak the language anyway. Understand what's being said in the interminable verbal jousting at family gatherings, understand what's said on TV, understand what's said behind her back at home. She feels excluded. Too fatigued, too lazy, too defenceless to plough on in spite of everything, including the lack of a means of transportation to get to the classes. She barely knows how to drive, is scared to do so, and it is out of the question that her husband send a ministry driver to satisfy her personal whims. She's never travelled as much abroad and felt so confined.

So Josée turns her attention entirely to my education. I become her passion, her happiness, her pledge of tenderness. The woman whose fragile health everyone laments is a marvellously imaginative mother who devotes herself to revealing to me the beauties of the world, a flower, a piece of music, a painting, a poem. She introduces me to her friends, as she says: to Schubert, Schumann, Fauré, Debussy and Bach that she teaches me to play on the magnificent piano my father gave her.

As a woman, however, she tightens up. The dissonance in her heart manifests itself in her body, in repeated bouts of cystitis, her aching back, her stomach that vomits this country's food. Mammo, an adorable man with an impossible character, grows increasingly tense. At home, he spits out the violence of power. Words become harsh, bodies close up. He runs from her. This she can understand. She's ashamed, blames herself, only natural that he abandons her, after all it's no fun having a wife who's always sick, but what can she do? Her only familiarity with health is in her search for it. She's been suffering so long she no longer knows how to live other than in her complaints. Neither I, nor he, nor this strange Ethiopia reduced to a house can do anything for her.

Her love turns into the folly of perfection, like a response to the collapse of the couple and of a body powerless to leave him. Save face, at all costs. She holds on, more and more tormented, a dinner to prepare, a bouquet to arrange, piano to practise. Tics contort her face. Mammo can't understand, why make such a fuss? He works like a madman, so many things to accomplish, so much inertia to combat, she has nothing to do, except what she imposes on herself. The obligation to conform to an admirable image against a body adrift. The accomplished wife of a great official. The perfect mother of a child who must be perfect too, to reflect an irreproachable education. Say hello to the lady, be the first in the class, use the proper cutlery, dress impeccably, immaculate socks stretched up over the knees, impeccable white shoes, hair tidily groomed in two braids held by beautiful white ribbons, with no frizzy strand escaping. Colour without going over the lines. Boundaries upon boundaries. A succession of golden enclosures. At bottom, she's suffocating. She is tired, so tired. Too afraid to step outside her self-imposed confines.

She cracks, he struggles, I yank my socks off. I adore walking barefoot.

Everything would have been simpler if Josée had frankly detested Ethiopia instead of loving it in spite of herself through Mammo, if they had been wrong once and for all, if it had been the fault of the West or of Africa, of the other forever other, of the other shore, of the other side. But nothing ever is. Because at the end of the day, it's always and primarily inside that things happen. In this distance from oneself for which we are accustomed to accusing the other.

My mother had always wanted to leave, and she had always come back. Out of love, weakness, fear of not being able to raise me alone in France, or for health reasons. This time, however, in December 1973, her decision seemed irrevocable. I was going on nine, was big enough, and she felt ready; we wouldn't come back after our visit to the family in Paris. A phone call from my father changed everything. Josée couldn't leave Mammo, not like this, not at the worst moment of his life. A few days before his arrest in the name of the revolution.

V

Echo Chamber

I feel like a tree
A tree caught
in the catacomb of bones
enslaved in
the red light districts of oppression
I feel like a barricade of trees
I feel like a tree

. . .

& sometimes
I feel like a tree
laughing in the rawness
of the wind

Jayne Cortez,
'Sacred Trees', *Somewhere in Advance of Nowhere*

Women, men, Black, white, children, old people, adults, national identity, religious identity, all this piling-up of categories, I don't know, I never have. These exhortations to be like this because of that, socks, straitjackets of the soul. Aren't we walking on the same Earth, under the same skies?

I owe to my parents my distrust of 'culture and country' alibi. It was through them that I approached that of Africa and Europe. History, geopolitics, everything written in capital letters begins and ends in the tiny retreat of a bedroom. It isn't continents, cultures or countries that thrash about in me, tugging at me from all sides, but presences. That of my mother, invasive, voluble, exclusive, and that of my father, silent, distant, confiscated. What was it to me to be Ethiopian or French when my interior mapping had been torn apart?

My perception of both countries is inseparable from the revolution, precisely because I'm from here and from there, and therefore displaced, with each country speaking of the absence of the other, of the impossibility of being in both at the same time. Without it, perhaps the existential duality that *métissage* brings to the front of the stage, in order to meditate on it, would not have been so inescapable. Without it, perhaps I would also have maintained the illusion of a duality of surface taken as a given, without delving further. I would have made do with it, as we are trained to do, out of intellectual as well as spiritual laziness, limping from incompleteness to incompleteness, without digging to its roots. In fracturing what had seemed to me to be inalienable, the revolution led me to probe the nature of a presence, a country, an affiliation, an attachment. Thus the important thing resided not so much in a difference due to the geographical and cultural divergence of my parents as in what was revealed by an event that was exterior to each of them. Without the revolution, my parents would have surely divorced for personal reasons, but on the pretext of cultural incompatibility. In separating them, the revolution led them to what united them. At least that is how I experienced it at first, my mother never having spoken of her husband as lovingly as during their separation, and he never having demonstrated as much tenderness as he did in his letters. Must we be separated to recognize what we loved?

I discovered this trait of the human psyche that makes us beings of desire and therefore of abandonment, not knowing how to appreciate what is given to us unless it is far away. Of course, at the time, that was not how I formulated or perceived it, filled as I was with empathy for my mother's grief that took precedence over mine. What I saw above all was that this revolution had given my mother the opportunity to rekindle a flame that daily life had nearly extinguished. I did not question her love for my father, but I was troubled by her elation. This woman who had never stopped complaining about him, until she decided to leave him, to leave a country whose language, food and music she didn't really enjoy, where she felt so lonely (I don't recall her having Ethiopian friends; acquaintances yes, but no intimate friendship), suddenly discovered an immense attachment to the man and his country. Was she in love with the man or with the landscape of her memories? With their love story or with the role of a brave and devoted heroine in which she had been cast by circumstances, in terror no doubt, but also with delight?

Who, at bottom, was this mother whom I was discovering as a woman, with her contradictions, her complexity and . . . alone? Isolated in this country of mine that was not hers, prey to demons that were not mine, and that I found myself having to face, alone. It was as if my father's absence had induced them to develop and make themselves at home. Fear, resentment, pride, possessiveness, fear again, fear most of all. Of debasement, of losing everything, of not having enough, of growing old, of staying, of leaving. Fear that one day I would slip away from her, that this country that had confiscated her husband in spirit, and now in the flesh, would take me away from her. Did she also fear that I would become too Ethiopian for her? I was all she had left. But who was I?

It was after our arrival in Paris that the full magnitude of these questions, initially dormant, came to surface. The adored mother, whose culture and beauty, artistic intelligence and anti-conformism I admired, and for whom I was always finding excuses, imputing the weight of her demons to circumstances, became a French-woman, and I, a *métis*. The one she criticized, when I displeased her, for being like my father, for *this* yes, all too Ethiopian.

No point in trying to pin down the *this* in question, the effec-tiveness of the gibe residing in its indeterminacy. The vaguer it was, the more disturbing it was, a bit like 'those people' who are not 'our kind of people': no one knows exactly who they are but you surely don't want to be one of them and you'll want to keep them at a dis-tance. In this case, it was my mother who felt distanced and side-lined. The reproach, I could clearly sense, served to deflect from her impotence. Her rage at not being able to control the child who was growing up was transferred to my foreign ancestry. All in all, it was basically just a change in scale in the very classic mechanism of making the other the source of a problem that concerns oneself alone. You are always the other one's child for your shortcomings. That the other is, in addition, from a foreign country only adds to the problem. Ah men or ah women, became in this case, ah

Ethiopians, who had nothing to do with it, of course, except to assume the brunt of her resentment.

Our disagreements took on continental proportions. We did not live in the same world any more. The necessary struggle of the teenager to set herself apart, get out from under her mother's wing and begin to develop her own identity, changed scales. From personal, it became collective. I no longer had to confront 'my' mother, but a whole series of clichés that exceeded us both. Ethiopians are proud, secretive, closed to others, their independence severed them from the world, they live in the past, incapable of forging ahead, unsuited to the realities of our times, what's more they don't know how to live. . . . Everything was mixed in, her personal grievances towards my father, her distress as a mother and woman, her fears for my future and for hers, and the burdens of the present.

Maybe my father hadn't wanted or known how to open the doors of his culture to her, to give her the keys that would have enabled her to decode many of the ways of behaving that baffled her? Maybe it was she who had never actually stepped over the threshold, a prisoner of her own prejudices or too lazy? And then Ethiopia, France, what? Who? Generalities are often used when things go wrong or to shirk our responsibility. No doubt this explains the difficulty of so-called mixed couples. The difference of the other forces us to ask ourselves who we are, and most of the time that is precisely what we don't want to do, given how comfortable it is to stick to codes that think for us. But these are considerations that are made from a *distance*, and for a moment, at that point of my adolescence, I felt betrayed. Deceived by a mother whom I did not recognize and who split me in two.

Where was the woman who had given me a taste for music, literature and the beauty of the world? The accomplice of the parties I invented to make her laugh, the one to whom I was bound by mutual love and trust?

It's one thing to see yourself as a foreigner and another to be described as such by your mother. And that's how it felt to me. Her reproaches had changed in nature. They were no longer aimed at my behaviour alone but at what I was, or, rather, was *not* any more in her eyes—namely, her child. My *métissage* had once been the fruit of an encounter, now it evoked an undesirable otherness. A part of me was designated as guilty. A part that I was being asked to hold in allegiance to another part, somewhat like an unruly lock that should be held in place. And that, by the way, is what happened. 'You are so much more beautiful when your hair is tied up,' she liked to say with just enough insistence to prompt me to leave my hair loose, less for me than to spite her. Aside from my hair being unruly, with regard to the laws of Western gravity and the straightness of its canons, there was the smell during my period, which needed all the more attention insofar as it was 'naturally' stronger in people 'like me'. I had the reflex to find such remarks silly, yet the feeling of unease toward my mother grew. Was she really speaking to me or to *something* through me? Was she really in control of what she was saying or under the influence of a certain *something*? Hmm, quite a bit of *something* in this business and although I didn't know exactly what or why, I could see the effects in my mother's eyes. With the kindness gone, they were the eyes of an accusing judge from whom I had to protect myself. I put out of reach that something in me they wanted to govern. My relationship with my father, with Ethiopia, and all that could have anything to do with it was buried away, sheltered from prying eyes. This became my secret garden, a silenced story, in the secrecy of my veins. At any rate, the imaginary and lexical words that were available (or might I say imposed) did not suit me. I neither wanted nor knew how to make what constituted me a subject of conversation.

All this might lead one to suppose that this open-minded, sensitive woman had turned into an abusive, racist mother, who scarred me for life. But not at all. She was hypocritical and possessive, to be sure, but she was mainly in a state of panic. Distraught for her child whom she now saw from the perspective of a white context. The very context that had made her afraid of giving birth to 'chequered children' and that she could not discern.

Blind spot.

The same old story again and again. We think we're addressing the other when ghosts are speaking through us.

Blind spot.

For her as much as for the teenager I was.

Blind spot: this context, never named as such, and which consequently had every latitude to impose itself as the sole possibility. The only reality. An order to which, if you wanted to survive, you had to submit, and prove your identity.

Blind spot: this *métissage* that somehow fell on me and in which I didn't recognize myself.

Question: Is one born *métisse* or does one become it through the force of a context?

Of a blind spot?

Something that would blur our vision, distorting perspectives and distances? A spot, a screen, that we could call border, race, nation, which we would take for realities, when they are merely optical illusions?

Perhaps the situation of the *métis* is to be the crucible of dual voices, sometimes complementary, sometimes discordant, which are the very fact of our humanity.

An echo chamber. In this sense, it is not so much a particular state, new and separate, as an underscored state. Its only specificity being to make more audible and visible what is already there in each of us. The duality of the interior and the exterior, of body and spirit, of the private and the political, of self and other, of my home and our home, of female and male, of shadow and light.

This at least was how I perceived the fact of being *métis*. I had to deal with the inside, through what was reflected back at me from outside, with the fact of being dual. This other that people with single identities, especially those who see themselves as such, tend to thrust far away, was inside me. To come back to the relationship with my mother, it was through exclusivity and the opposition it generates, rather than through race, that I approached this question of *métissage*.

Although I hated her possessiveness and cultural arrogance, she was nonetheless the mother I loved and I the daughter she loved 'more than anything in the world'. Lest I live mutilated or in perpetual internal warfare, by the choice of one ancestry over another, I could not take her aberrant comments at face value. I had to understand them, and to do so, I had to go back to their source. I had no choice. My *métissage* compelled me to do so. I was obliged to delve deeper, if I wanted to come out whole. This geographic and sensitive duality of perception and apprehension of the world, which I discovered in the gaze of my mother, became an invitation to question. To look for a meaning for what it meant to be *métis*. Not from outside but from within.

If we stick to the outside, it's simple. As I have shown, the *métis* exists only as a product of racial division. Consequently, the person thus designated will have to deal with this division, more or less so depending on the place where she finds herself. In this sense, the hybridity of the *métis* is transgressive not fusional in nature. It bespeaks a monstrosity instead of leading to the abolition of racial boundaries. There is no such thing as *métis* without race, and no such thing as race without a political agenda. Therefore, it is this agenda that must be examined rather than the artificial racial question, since all that can be said about the *métis* proceeds from its interests. The abstruse convolutions of the French Academy to hang on to *métis*, while trying to drop race like hot potato, is proof thereof. Difficult not to throw out the baby with the bath water, especially when you have a hard time distinguishing the two because you yourself are in the bath.

If we stick to the outside, hence to the political sphere, there can be no *métis* subject, in both senses of the term, since the latter is nothing but a fictional construct in the service of colonial domination. The vocabulary may have changed but not the subject. Whether the existence of the *métis* is reviled or promoted, it is always as a function of the interests of the dominant power alone. Step over the fence if you like, as long as it stays in place. Prohibiting *métissage* in the name of racial purity or extolling its qualities ultimately boils down to the same thing. It's always a question of race and from the point of view of a single one. It's not the model that changes but the strategy. To avoid straining the rudder to breaking point, one must adapt to the currents of history. Domination first, domination always, and therein the notion of *métissage* can only have a sinister resonance. No meeting or conversation is possible here, no other alternative than the profanation or obliteration of one race by the other. Whether it serves as an instrument of revenge or finds itself contributing, in spite of itself, to the aims of a eugenic project—the well-known whitening of the race in the West Indies, to take just one example—the *métis*, in this context, cannot exist for itself.

Blind spot and full stop.

If, in my case, I stick to this outside, it's very simple. As an Afro-European *métis*, I am Black to whites and white to Blacks. Basically. No need to go into details, it's a well-known story, hashed and rehashed. If you don't want to spend your time complaining from one side or the other, I don't really see what there is to say about it

And yet here I am. If I stick to this, to the simple fact of existing in life, this outside that seemed so vast as to be inescapable, this outside that seemed to condemn me from the outset to being nothing but its toy, becomes very small. A minuscule part of what we call reality. Even if it plays a big part in it.

Maybe what is true for all of us was underscored in my case. Not because I was *métis*, but because I was an artist. And maybe that's where it all started. A conflict of realities. A shift of perception. A crack.

I ate, talked, breathed cinema, theatre, freedom; my mother hammered home reality, reality, reality. Sales at the supermarket, anxiety at making ends meet every month, the dread of new beginnings, bills to pay, work, two-hour subway commutes every day, calluses on her feet, aches in her back, cold in her heart, the letters that piled up to apply for a scholarship, to demand my father's release, the queues, the administration, the paperwork, again the paperwork and this damn teen who thought of nothing but theatre.

'You'd like to rise to the heights of Bach and Rimbaud, but that's not reality,' was the mantra my mother would pound at me like a jackhammer. But Bach and Rimbaud had indeed lived, and wasn't she the one who gave me a taste for them? Leaving aside Bach and Rimbaud, who were friends among others, not models, and who had nothing to do with the matter, why was she talking to me about heights? Was art a jar of jam to be put away at the top of a cupboard? At the bottom, a tangible existence, therefore necessarily bland and grey, and at the top, its flavourful fruit? A reality split horizontally, with one floating above, the other in its shadow below, disconnected. No elevation possible, just the prospect of getting a stiff neck. And yet, doesn't the wonder of the flower well up from the depths of the earth? Vertically?

No, I definitely did not recognize my mother any more. But thanks to her, I began to make out the contours of this something that was being expressed through her. This something that had first divided her and had reached me by ricochet, so to speak. A something that also bothered me outside, pervading the atmosphere with a dry and trenchant quality. A something that grew over the years and which, after confusing it with my mother, I attributed to France.

Poetry here remained locked in books. The poetry I hadn't read in Amharic, not because it didn't exist but because I had no access to it, was also unfolding in space in Ethiopia. I could decipher it in bodies. Here in Paris, it seemed to me to have retreated. The way people had of moving, their way of being or, rather, of not being, gave me the impression of a disembodied environment. Dry. The setting was perhaps magnificent, the architecture splendid, to me the atmosphere of the city felt angular. As was its temporality, compressed, reduced from the cycle of the stars and their light to that of clocks. A one-note ticking. In the harmonics, the rhythms, the textures. From six-eight to binary. From a time that inspires, suspends and bounces, a pulse that makes room for the invisible, to a beat that crushes you to the ground.

Yet it was here that what was important to me became possible. Including the study of my silenced language, the paternal Amharic. But the dryness of the university could give me only the husk.

I was cold. My father, my native land, were wrapped in the enchanting mirages that distance confers.

One reality versus the other. Until the phone rang.

The voice from a distance of my aunt Mary shouting:

—Hello, Josée?

—No, it's Myriam.

—Myriam! He's free! Mammo is free! Free!

The sky opened up.

Elation lifted me up.

I danced.

The clamp of nine years of confinement popped like a champagne cork.

Through my father I was going to be reunited with that part of me left over there. Thanks to him, I was going to walk on both legs. Everything would be fine again. Balanced . . .

I was eighteen when my father came to France, a year after his release. The year of my first steps as a woman and an actor, the year I walked through the door of the National Institute for Oriental Languages and Civilizations (INALCO) so I could walk in my two languages. I thought it would please him that I'd studied the history of Ethiopia, taken up the thread of his expression, mine, ours, that he'd see it as a sign of affection and interest in him, an outstretched hand to start a conversation . . . 'A waste of time' was my father's cutting response. 'You'd do better to study something more useful. Nobody talks in Amharic outside Ethiopia. It won't do you much good. What you know is more than enough.'

Slap in the face. Sorrow mingled with joy, doubt with tenderness, absence with presence. Did he really have such little regard for his language and for my need to enter it and not simply to get by? What did he know anyway, when he'd never addressed a word to me in any language but French? Four lines in Amharic, that was the limit of our exchanges during the four years of his imprisonment, followed by silence for four more. Didn't he understand that he was the one I was seeking through this language?

Anger. Like a child who is sent to play outside whenever a conversation turns serious. The impression of being rejected and excluded. Twice uprooted. First when I was wrenched from my native land and, now, by my father withholding his words from me.

Who did he take me for? A student looking for a career path, wagering on a language like you would bet on a racehorse? What good was his blood without the song of his word, in exile from his verb?

Disconcerted, disappointed, distressed, I held my peace. He was coming out of prison and I out of an adolescence deprived of his presence. He and I were equally clumsy in our belated reunion. He was concerned about my future and I was trying to find my identity. The one I thought I'd lost when I slipped out of his lexicon.

Orders and devouring of identity.

What was at stake with this language to which I'd attached such importance? The assurance of being Ethiopian or of being accepted? 'You're repudiating your blood,' my classmate in Ethiopia had reproached me when I stopped taking Amharic classes. Wasn't it this curse that had pursued me? I had to prove, to reassure myself that I was truly Ethiopian, since people in France were always referring me back to this and to what could be questionable in my native country. I don't deny the feelings and personal interest that motivated me, the question is not there. It is in this need of proof. Not only by default—after all, fracture characterizes us all—but also by what is specific to the situation of the *métis*: namely, the injunction of loyalty.

The *métis* is the one through whom the other irrupts from within. The one who disturbs the familiar by this air of not from here. Not utterly foreign but not quite the same either. As is often the case with what is not clearly identifiable, she creates a malaise.

The hybridity makes her suspect, because you never really know who you're dealing with and towards which side she leans. This is not so much a matter of race as of boundaries. The *métis*, by her familiar (and I might say familial) uncanniness, not only transgresses those boundaries, she pulverizes them. And that is much more disturbing. How can you feel safe and secure in your existence without them? How can you avoid the risk of being overwhelmed by the other and disappearing? Be it only a figment of the imagination, many identities cling to the idea of their impermeability. And that is the problem. Wherever she finds herself, the *métis* knows she is also of the other. Intrinsically. Which makes her not so much more flexible as often discomfiting and discomfited. It isn't easy to have one foot outside, in a world in which you are asked to lock the door. Under pressure, the *métis* is often led to put more weight on the foot inside. To show, to prove, to reassure others that she is here, wholly here, despite the other in her. In a word, that she is not playing a double game.

This demand for loyalty has no doubt changed in degree and in nature since the creation of the *métis* by the colonizing West. It is nonetheless omnipresent in the collective unconscious. As the child of an encounter, a mix of peoples, the *métis* embodies the disorder of desire in the order of nations. The less self-confident do not appreciate this. As for individuals, it all depends on whether or not they identify with the nation in question. If the two poles are in open conflict, the affection of the *métis* child for one or the other may be seen as a betrayal by both sides, as in a divorce situation. A catalyser for antagonistic forces, the *métis* is under pressure from both, and must all too often pay the cost of social integration with schizophrenia, or else stifle one identity in favour of the other. Since the duality cannot be a conjunction, it becomes a subtraction.

This was not the case for me and yet, even though I defended myself against it, the designation had trapped me. Believing myself free, I was chained to the fear of being confined or rejected. Hard to resist the need to belong. What is a country and an identity when everything comes to you in duplicate? Or, rather, what's left of them? The fatality of being a *métis* in a society that looks at you in terms of your absent country: one plus one equals zero, not two.

The misunderstanding was salutary in this respect. My father's deafness to my call put me in my place. Why try to reassure myself about what I was already? What need did I have of holding onto this Ethiopian identity as if it were an exterior object? Ethiopia for whom? From what point of view? That of a France where it had to be constantly explained or that of the child who had been wrested from it?

What my father wanted to keep me away from was not his language but his wound. What good are words without the tenderness of their land? Irretrievably lost in his case, infinitely sought in mine. He was seeing as one who is in exile, I was begging as one who's been uprooted.

Country, belonging, identity, all this chatter quieted down little by little. Here we were, facing each other, by each other's side, and we could talk. Wasn't that all that mattered? He, my father, and I, his child.

Métis? A word he'd never uttered and would never pronounce.

I'm twenty years old. In the eyes of French society, my father is Black and I'm not Black enough. He is imprisoned in his exile, my mother is walled up in her complaints. I stand in the middle. As usual. The child of a discordant encounter.

'Damn it! I've had it with Ethiopia! Always the same thing . . . Enough already. It's time to turn the page. Live for God's sake!'

She isn't wrong. I understand my mother. All these years spent fighting, preparing, hoping for her husband's release, for his return, struggling to find shelter for their new life, one flat after another, one move after another, a place to proudly arrange what she had managed to save from our shipwreck, for us, for them, with so much courage, work, love and now . . . . He, continually talking about an Ethiopia that exists no more, and she, crying over a new possibility that is not coming to fruition.

My father, too, I understand. A country is not a page that can be turned, especially in a France that obliterates you when you wear it on your skin. Nothing here to spark a desire to throw himself into being and do whatever it takes, when earlier he was someone. In spite of all, he struggles, for her sake. And then his country is not an accident in his life, it is his whole life.

It's always the same story. Two people living in the ongoing conflict of their presence. Their day-to-day life does not seem to withstand the dream they had of each other. A question of countries or the eternal problem of couples?

My father's Ethiopia is no longer, my mother's France is an illusion. I understand both of them without seeing myself in them. My *métissage* is a division of times. The blind spot of the present.

Injunctions and illusions of identity.

So many walls for a spot in the universe.

I'm twenty-five and I refuse to surrender my presence to the spectres of colour.

I hunger for other stories and other spaces. I need an 'us' with which to invent a present that isn't intercepted by high voltage lines of memory. An 'us' that is an invention rather than a reproduction. An 'us' of the spirit. From this France that adores speaking about humanity but regards what does not resemble itself as a less or a too much for itself.

I quit Rue Blanche and start a theatre troupe with friends. It so happens that they come from the African continent. Clearly I've taken a wrong turn. I haven't a chance of succeeding as far as my mother is concerned, and every chance of being taken for ride as far as my father is concerned.

The world of the actor being what it is, namely, white, I have every interest in adapting to it. Dressing in a suit rather than in exotic clothes, having straight hair rather than those, what are they again? dreadlocks? ... whatever ... and choosing decent people to spend time with. Make an effort and don't shut yourself up in a ghetto. Which is always Black and never white, of course, but that's my malicious spirit speaking. France is the country of the Rights of Man and of the Enlightenment, don't forget it, and if it shits on you, it's necessarily because you were in the wrong place, even if it put you there by invading your country—there's my malicious spirit speaking again. So, adapt. Emphasize my French ancestry, and hang onto it like a lifeline. It may be ugly and sad, but it's the only way not to sink in 'this, alas, racist society', says my mother.

That isn't the question for my father. His concern is that I don't forget my identity, which is Ethiopian, not African. Don't confuse the two. I should not take on the problems of ex-colonized people who, no matter what they say, have remained just that. They're not trustworthy. Their minds have been spoiled. He knows a thing or two about it. God knows how he worked with all his might for this long-hoped-for pan-Africanism, he doesn't want me to think otherwise. Ethiopia always sided with the freedom fighters, the first to sever diplomatic relations with South Africa, to support the ANC, founder of the OAU, ever ready to stick out its neck, like for the Palestinian cause, but, hey, that was a different matter altogether. In concrete terms, all the cooperation that he'd tried to establish had failed due to internal divisions. Greed, egotism, pettiness. The great figures had been assassinated. Only the lackeys of Western power remained. That's not the point and I'm not in politics? As if the latter had no impact on people's behaviour. He's afraid that I'll be taken for a ride, especially by these francophones. Dumbed down by French-style assimilation. No manners. A few hard heads, it's true. But when it comes to getting together to do something, zilch. Ready to kill one another for the crumbs thrown their way. Alas. No, I mustn't get mixed up with them.

So what next? What do we do? Cry? Lie down in the grave that our elders dug from their defeats? To begin with, I don't spend time with Africans but with people, artists whose sensibilities coincide with mine. Ethiopia who? Which Africa? Does he realize that with his them and us, he is reproducing exactly what he condemns? And then what? Am I going to spend the rest of my life intelligently criticizing the system, blaming a global 'them' for my aborted vocation, and end up a victim, doomed never to take my life in my own hands?

My mother cries: 'I should never have made you a *métis*. The world was not ready for it.'

I keep quiet.

Cruel misunderstanding of worlds. That of the living and that of colour.

Wasn't I born a girl, not a *métis*?

What world made me the subject of a misunderstanding?

Ubuntu. I am because we are.

Where?

I go from one misunderstanding to another. My mother thinks I'm against her and all French people when I criticize a system obsessed with colour. My father thinks I distrust them when I protect myself from their fears. I was hoping for an us of creation, but it exists only in reaction. My Africa was spiritual, in France it is identified with a colour. Imprisoned in the eyes of the West. The shadow of race covers us like a glue. We struggle to escape it, desperately seeking to emerge into the light. The more we fight it, the stronger the power of the shadow grows, gnawing at our lives like a curse. A Gorgon shadow. Where can we find the mirror that would show it its own reflection.

The fact that race is the product of a Western narrative devised for its predatory needs explains the motives behind its manufacture, but says nothing about the nature of the West and its hold on us all, even into the heart of our bedrooms. Furthermore, making it into the sole disease of Europeans amounts to letting ourselves be conceived in its terms and perceiving ourselves as nothing but victims.

These misunderstandings echo a fault line within philosophy that I'd perceived during my studies. On the one hand, a family of thinkers situated on the side of the living, the moving, the converging; on the other, a family of system conceptualizers, paranoid and rigid. I'm going to tell you about the world, but I start by suspending it to conceptualize it (Descartes, for example). The latter had supplanted the former and, as in history, there was domination of one world over the other. The forces of power had prevailed over the *marronage* of thought, the political over the poetic. This reading had 'saved' me at the time from racism by enabling me not to assimilate all Europeans to the making of race. Because the horrors committed in its name had left me questioning. All the more given that they continued to be perpetrated, by the same people, in South Africa. Who were these human beings, I asked myself at the time, who had the gall to see themselves as discoverers of a world which hadn't waited for them to exist and which was still bleeding from their macabre madness? I didn't think that other peoples were exempt from this—history in all latitudes and at all times demonstrates as much—but it seemed to me that no other had reached such a degree of absolute horror, arrogating the right to exterminate and enslave entire continents on its own behalf, establishing itself not as master—this remained within the realm of normalcy, within the bounds of a human taste for power and material possession—but as superior race. Powerful, so powerful it even exceeded monotheistic supremacies. This poor God, in whose name people were exterminating one another, had simply created the world and its inhabitants, and along came a small delusional group and they took it in their heads to create race. A single race above all: God, the world and its inhabitants. Because there was one and only one in the end, the others serving only to legitimate it, to make it exist. I could not believe that light-skinned men, having become white, ever took other races seriously—their scientific posturing about there being other (sick but human) races, notwithstanding; on the other hand, they clung to their own. They seemed no longer able to do without it. Were they so afraid of disappearing without it? This was not the case, however, for all Europeans. Far from it. So were they the exception that confirmed the rule?

The plurality of thinking that I discovered in my philosophy studies helped me at the time to avoid mistaking the target. The question was not the Europeans and their disease, but their identification with this evil. Hadn't this shadowy part of Europe begun eating away at it, like a plague destroying entire civilizations in its path?

Gorgon shadow. Didn't its power reside in holding us in its thrall, blind to us, all?

Some years ago, as we were about to leave each other after an interview, a young woman asked me: 'Do you prefer to speak of yourself as *métis* or African?' I was dumbfounded. Coming from someone whose mother was French and father Malian, the question was ludicrous, to say the least. I could understand if she'd asked me with which country I have more affinities, even though I don't appreciate this type of question because, on the one hand, it re-enacts the racial division of the *métis* by forcing a choice, and, on the other, it reduces the shifting complexity of intimate relations to a Manichean binarity. But to oppose two terms, the one including in our case the other, is nonsensical, if not downright absurd. What was it all about? Rejecting a problematic label for another that was no less problematic? What preference could one have when the constraint is the same, namely, having to speak of oneself in terms of a designation that one did not choose? Why would anyone feel not only resigned but compelled to do so? To call myself 'African' in opposition to '*métis*' amounted in this case to settling scores with France, on Africa's back. As usual. Wasn't it high time to stop participating in, and thereby endorsing, the terms of an identity seen from the sole standpoint of asserting rights?

Shifting from one appellation to another within the same framework resolves nothing. Because the problem is the framework itself.

I thought again of my mother's words: 'I should never have made you a *métis*. The world was not ready for it.' She'd uttered them out of despair, and initially I'd felt hurt and then furious, but I also saw the love in them, her prayer for a world delivered from its chains. Who forged the links of this chain, generation after generation, if not every one of us, with words that go against our beings?

No, I could not resign myself to such a preference in speaking of myself under the tyranny of a partial conception (in both senses of the term) of myself. And anyway, what need is there to be something when you're a person?

'Nothing,' I replied.

VI

The Way to the Self

. . . I replaced the dictionary by my heart.

Mahmoud Darwish,
'Chroniques de la douleur palestinienne'[7]

I am what I am through what we are all, according to Ubuntu philosophy. Being *métis* for me meant learning to embody this, to understand it, by experiencing the wound of this divided us. A role, among others, that I took as such. Not to settle into it but for what is to be learnt from living through it.

The history of the term *métis* and the ugliness that spawned it are not mine. I do not see myself in them. I am a child of life, not of race. Yet I had to bear this word, tainted by this curse. To examine the misunderstandings that it revealed as to what we are, what we all are. Living beings destined to grow in awareness. Isn't that what the tales of initiation have been telling us since time out of

---

7 Translated from the French, in *Rien qu'une autre année* (Paris: Les Éditions de minuit, 1983).

mind? So many stories, like pebbles strewn on the path, to guide our steps through the forest of our emotions. And we cling to the worst, the most poorly constructed one, which leads to nothing but itself. A story that goes round in circles. Cursed, in that it has nothing to say. A commentary on its own prattle. Hollow. A sham that feeds on the reality that we lend to it, to the detriment of our own.

I am by what we are. But how can I be when this 'we' has been emptied of its substance and replaced by a figment of the imagination, namely, a racial category? Because race does not exist—that's a fact—outside the gaze of the West. And this would be inoperative without the eyes we yield to it. Seeing a person as Black or white does not refer to a skin colour but to the discourse associated with it. What is being perceived in this case is not a colour, let alone a human being, but, rather, a political hologram. A projection that annihilates everyone. As much the person thus designated, who is replaced by a mirage, as the person who thinks she's seeing, and who is enslaved to the function of a projector. No one is there.

It is understood that race is a narrative fabricated by the West for its predatory purposes, but the power it has to ceaselessly divide us is our common responsibility. Were we to remove it from our vocabulary, it would resurface in other forms, like a disease whose symptoms alone have been masked. Whether we think of ourselves as racists or antiracists amounts in this sense to the same thing. In either case we are still driven by the notion of race and mired in the same unconscious. Its manifestation is undoubtedly political, but what causes it results from a spiritual problem. A distortion of the spirit. Hence, combatting race on its own basis, meaning that of division, will not deliver us from its grip. On the contrary, all it will do is continue to feed it.

I am by what we *all* are. Race is the perversion of this 'we' of relation into a 'we' of prostration. It's we the women, we the men, we the poor, we the rich, we x religion, we z religion, we Blacks, we whites, we the dominated, we the dominators, and so on and so forth. An escalation of 'we's' on a bloodlet humanity. Until the extinction of this world that sustains and welcomes us.

It's not race that kills, it's our resignation. It's we, insofar as we are absent from what we are: part of the universe. We, becoming prey to our identifications, when we delegate the exclusivity of our identity to them for the sake of having one. We, hypnotized by the malignant force of power that separates us limb from limb into colours, castes, classes, nations, religions, and that seizes our life force.

I am what I am by what we all are. No adjectives here, a single verb. From the self to the other and the other to the self. Being.

No, I am not a *métis*. I am.

It's a requirement of responsibility.

A journey.

A story . . .